Retire Happy:

Retired and Inspired Retirement Your Way!

Live by your own rules.

Retiring?
The Ultimate Mature Lifestyle Planning Guide

For people who want to live life to the fullest.

Kristi Nielsen
Retirement Coach

What Did You Think of *Retire Happy!*
First of all, thank you for purchasing this book. If you enjoyed this book, it would be really nice if you could share this book with your friends and family by posting to Facebook and Twitter.

I hope that you could take some time to post a review on Amazon. Your feedback and support will help the author to make future books better. Your review is very important and so, if you'd like to leave a review, on Amazon. While you are there check out other books by *Kristi Nielsen.*
Thanks again! I appreciate your support!

Dedicated to My Family -- In memory of my father, who lived life to its fullest and who was young at heart. To my cherished children, it is a privilege to have you in my life—always has been, always will be. To my grandchildren who still don't know the power of their choices. You are the sunshine that bears the hope of the future.

Canadian Cataloguing in Publication Data 1. Retirement – Planning 2. Financial – Personal 3. Quality of Life 4. Quality of Worklife 5. Lifestyles – Economic Aspects

I Title

Retire Happy:
Retired and Inspired - Retirement YOUR Way!
Live by Your Own Rules
Paperback: ISBN: 978-1-989607-19-0
E-Book: ISBN: 978-1-989607-20-6

Table of Contents

CHAPTER 1

IS RETIREMENT PASSÉ?

RETHINKING TERMINOLOGY

Retirement at sixty-five is ridiculous. When I was sixty-five I still had pimples.

George Burns (1896 - 1996)

At age 45 you possibly have another 45 years to create this adventure called life. If you are 65 and reading this, you could have another 30 years left to live. Just think of all the things you have done in the past decade; experiences that have enriched you as a person, giving you a cornerstone on which to build an astounding retirement. The best is yet to come…what will it be?

Lamenting about one's chronological age is a waste of time and talent. Life at any age is the cumulative result of our decisions, actions and responses to circumstances. What is your definition of ideal retirement and what is the key to enjoying it? Does the word 'retirement' even fit?

By now you should have the maturity to make choices based on increased self-knowledge; what fuels your passions and what means most to you. This book will examine how understanding transition, managing change, and engaging in an exploration process can normalize the anxieties you may feel as you approach retirement.

We will share inspiring stories of people who have created a meaningful retirement. The process will include the challenge of determining what we as individuals really want, what brings meaning to our lives and how to convert our retirement dreams into reality.

Beyond Boomers

For decades people born between 1946 and 1964 were referred to as the Baby Boomers. The term *'baby'* should never be use to refer to an adult of any age. Thankfully we have stopped using this term, for the most part.

So many aspects of the dialogue used to discuss the aging process and retirement do not fit people born after WWII. The historical meaning of the term *seniors* does not fit for this demographic, whether they are 65 or 70 or even 75.

People born after WWII are distinctly different from any previous generation at the same age, need their own word to describe the lifestyle-transitions they are about to enter. Traditional words, such as *retirement* and *seniors*, and their meanings don't fit.

Retirement is an archaic word not matching the lifestyle most people who are past 60-years-of-age today. According to the Merriam Webster Dictionary: **Retirement** \ri-ˈtī(-ə)r-mənt\ *noun* Date: 1596 **1 a**: an act of **retiring :** the state of being **retired b:** withdrawal from one's position or occupation or from active working life **c:** the age at which one normally **retires** <reaches *retirement* in

May> **2**: a place of seclusion or privacy

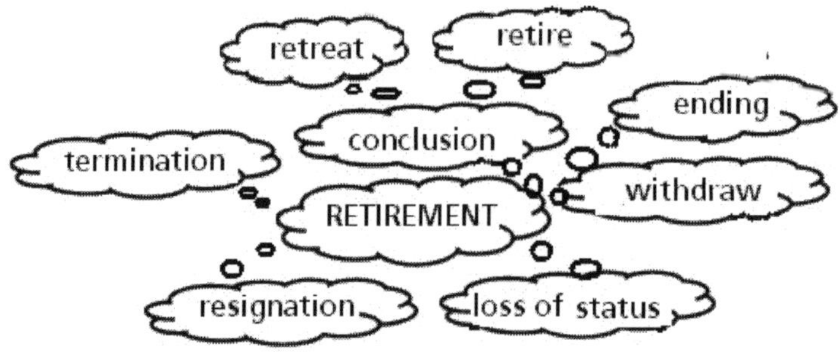

None of these definitions match the paradigm of retirement held by this generation. Old retirement definitions evoke visions of granny in a rocking chair and grandpa snoring on the couch, having fallen asleep reading the newspaper.

The new generation of retirees is a group of physically active, well-educated, financially powerful people involved in the shaping of our nation. This generation envisions luxury vacations, leisurely carefree lifestyles, the continuation of work on a full-or part-time basis, and active involvement in the community.

Retirement, a word originating in 1596, seems unfitting to describe a life stage for the Plus 50 demographic. We are a group of keen people transitioning through a phase of life defined by dreams and visions, not by age. We are rejecting the

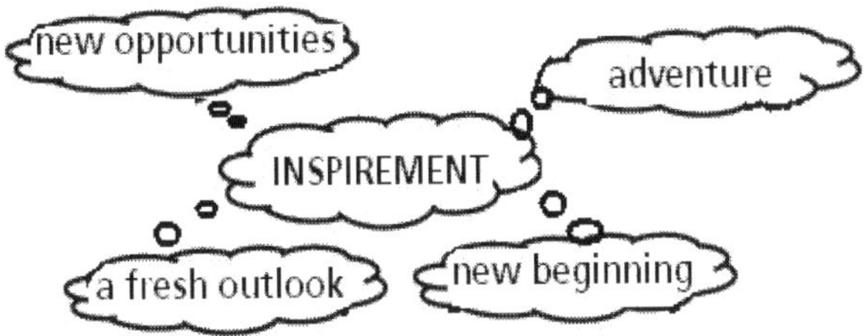

old model of retirement in exchange for a new model that I prefer to describe as *Inspirement***.** They are inspiring people entering a time of life filled with inspiring opportunities.

Old retirement was an event–the gold watch and a big party usually followed by a non-eventful life. New retirement is not an end, but a new beginning filled with exciting new life experiences and a series of transitions. Boomers are moving through a variety of phases where independence, fulfillment, and lifestyle are their greatest motivators.

There is an expectation that those approaching this transition should have all the answers to all the dilemmas they may face over the next 30 to 55 years. For some, the crystal ball shows a crossroads between a hectic, often chaotic life and a life filled with relaxation, pleasure and financial freedom.

The crystal ball falls short of being able to accurately predict all the changes that lay ahead on both a personal and societal level. The series of transitions between mid-life and our mid-seventies, define and shape our remaining productive years, and may or may not lead to bonus years.

For many, the end of life may occur, sometimes suddenly, during active retirement, while for others whose physical and mental functioning leads to l'età dell'oro (Italian for Golden Age), the utility of life begins to ebb. Yet, even in the bonus years, the wisdom of many seniors escalates them to become all too often unappreciated sages with much to share.

As retirement implies a single event, a, much more appropriate word is *segue*. According to the

Merriam Webster Dictionary: **se·gue**: 'se-(")gwA, 'sA- *verb imperative* **1:** proceed to what follows without pause -- used as a direction in music **2:** perform the music that follows like that which has preceded -- used as a direction in music.

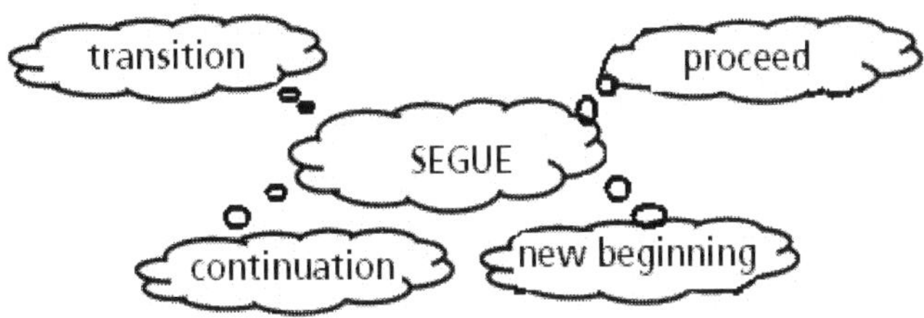

Dictionary.com also offers "any smooth, uninterrupted transition from one thing to another" (*Dictionary.com Unabridged (v 1.1)*.

Retirement, or at least the first half of it, can be more accurately replaced with *Segue Years*—a period when people between 50 and 75 or even 80 are in a sustained segue. Creating the new term *Segue Years* allows a modern description of the process.

Segue Years (pronunciation: **sĕg**'wā'-yirs **sey**-gwey-' yirs, **seg**-wey- yirs ') noun **1.** a natural transition occurring with relative ease leading toward increased independence and fulfillment, from traditional or life-long employment to increased recreation, leisure and lifestyle changes which may or may not include some form of income generation **2.** A life stage spanning from the later end of mid-life to the bonus years.

Using this term throughout this book is intended to establish a new understanding of the process of a decreased career development phase, moving toward increased independence and a stage of life focused on life-meaning.

However, anyone grounded in reality knows retirement is not always so idyllic. Approaching retirement can cause many mixed emotions; it may evoke questions that cause anxiety; the very idea of retirement may send a shiver of fear through to your bones.

Preparation for retirement involves much more than financial readiness–attempts to define financial preparedness can be fraught with more questions than answers. This stage of life is further complicated by changing trends as our generation confronts and challenges the traditional model of retirement, accepted by previous generations. We are seeking to redesign the way our society looks at the second half of life–opting for a fuller, more active life.

Retirement will bring varied challenges for every individual, as do their present circumstances. While it is often said that this generation is approaching retirement far wealthier and better prepared than previous generations, the actual fact is that never before has there been such a contrast between the rich and the poor–as in this generation of retirees.

Many employee pensions have disappeared; the likelihood of government-funded pensions seems, at best, insecure. The gap between those who *have* and those who *have not* begs the question: How much does it take to put you among the *haves*?

Often homeowners forget the value of their asset when viewing their financial status. The division between the *haves* and the *have nots* often begins with the financial security that property ownership brings. Even the cash-strapped property-rich rank among the *haves*.

Unless those who are not property owners have massive investments and pensions, they become *have nots* in desperate need of a plan to survive. Other factors that alter the reality of retirement are perceptions of *how much is enough* and all the questions relating to retirement lifestyle. We will discuss these topics later in this book.

The first time in life that we undergo a major life-changing transition is our teenage years, during which we make many decisions about who we are and our future goals. As we approach retirement; we undergo an equal or larger life-changing transition.

We re-evaluate who we are, our life purpose, goals, contributions to society, values, and how we are going to spend our time on a day-to-day basis. We face the danger of drifting into an abyss where our time fills with trivialities like vacuuming and mowing the lawn more often, and flicking the TV remote; or we can choose to engage in full, active, meaningful living.

The *dream retirement* doesn't belong to dreamers – successful, meaningful retirement lifestyles belong to those who are engaged in the process of *positive doing*.

The *dream retirement* doesn't belong to dreamers– successful, meaningful retirement lifestyles belong to those who are engaged in the process of *positive doing*. Dreams only become reality when we take actions that support what we envision.

It requires strategy, an understanding of the transition process, skills to break through perceived barriers, and a willingness to engage fully in the process. Needless to say, those who sacrifice day-after-day of their lives awaiting the day that nirvana will come to sweep them from their complacent state into a new reality—find that it never happens.

They live out their final days in a state of disillusionment. A life worth living doesn't happen spontaneously–it is the product of enlightened decisions, clear focus, and consistent engagement in *positive doing* while investing in our personal life purpose.

Retirement is no longer an event–it is unlikely that you will leave your career with the gold watch and a big party. Retirement is more accurately an ongoing process. There is no correct time to start this process. While resigning from one's career may be a marker event, termination of one's career does not necessarily mean retirement has occurred.

The discussion about retirement covers opportunities, options, challenges, effective strategies and the transition process. We need to be cognizant of the magnitude and variety of our life experiences during the first half of our lives, realizing the second half of our lives has the potential of being filled with diverse experiences, accomplishments, and adventures.

Amazing stories about the lives of retirees, which we will share later, provide you with every reason for optimism and an adventurous spirit. Even as the first half of your life has brought unforeseeable events, so will the second half. You are the one who is writing your own life story. Most events that come into our lives result from our own choices. Accept the responsibility for your decisions and actions wherever possible. Accept responsibility for how you react to those things that are beyond your control.

Human beings are vulnerable. When tragedies happen and we are often impacted by situations beyond our control, our reaction is within our control. As we age, the inevitability of depreciating health and the reality of our mortality can result in preoccupation with thoughts that rob us of our ability to enjoy the present. Developing a healthy attitude toward life's darker side is crucial to your well-being. You need a bushel-basket full of courage, tenacity and resilience to sustain you through life's difficult experiences.

Our ability to cope with problems increases as life becomes a teacher, providing us with new opportunities to practice each year. We develop resilience, a better understanding of self and others, and *change management* skills useful for the latter half of our lives. Celebrating one's accomplishments and recognizing retirement as a life stage rather than an event are clearly the best choices.

The benefits of aging are many. As we age, we gain wisdom–something just not available to us in our youth. We develop skills to manage difficult experiences, stress, interpersonal conflict and communication.

Maturity, as viewed by psychologists, is the move toward individuality and self-acceptance. The opportunity to celebrate our individuality is the ultimate freedom. It separates us from the anxiety of worrying that we will not measure up to other people's expectations. As we learn to accept our own mistakes and laugh at them, we learn to accept ourselves for who we authentically are and can enjoy ourselves more.

Archaic Concepts of Retirement

The old definition of retirement focuses on end of life. Retirement was the value of live fading away with a fatal end. With this as a paradigm it shouldn't be surprising that the death rate of men spiked in the first few years after their retirement. Those who made it through the first few years after retirement lived on, and death rates leveled out.

Retirement therefore has a very fatalistic connotation. It isn't surprising we want to replace this with something more meaningful.

Additionally, religion has loaded us with the huge burden of reconciling our feeling regarding the end of life. Religious teachings, for some, evoke fears of the Judgment Day, or Hell. While many religious people say they believe in Heaven, it seems it brings them little solace. We have an innate desire to live—on earth for as long as we can. Of course during our life on earth, we want health and earthly comforts.

There can be a reluctance to talk about death because we may associate it with the tremendous loss of a loved one. Most of us spend very little time thinking about or discussing our beliefs about the afterlife. There are no answers and it seems to be our nature to want concrete answers.

Failure to become comfortable talking about death results in an inability to support one another when a friend or relative passes. People try to comfort grieving family members and feel totally lost for words, in part because so many of us have varying views on what happens after life on earth ends.

It is baffling that many people who claim to believe in Heaven–and even a reunion with loved ones in Heaven–still seem to be uncomfortable with death. This may be why more families are embracing Celebration of Life events in lieu of funerals. Celebrating one's life seems more comforting and less focused on loss.

If they see death as only a temporary separation from a loved one, why is it so difficult to accept? If one fears to die–one settles for fearing to live. Death is inevitable-you may as well take a few risks and really learn to live life to the fullest—before and during retirement.

Traditional definitions of retirement invoke thoughts of failing physical and mental well-being culminating with the end of life. Modern concepts of retirement suggest retirement is, rather, part of the continuum of life–marked by numerous transitions leading to a renewal and expansion of the meaningfulness of life.

Overcoming negative connotations relating to death and developing a healthy attitude toward death–as a normal part of the human experience--is beneficial to mental well-being.

Celebrate Mid-Life: Jungian Archetypes and Mid-Life Spirituality by Janice Brewi and Anne Brennan identifies four births: physical birth, puberty, mid-life and death, with each birth leading into something bigger. Based on this philosophy, puberty is the birth to adulthood and sexuality; mid-life hurls one into life meaning and death is a birth into the afterlife.

It is more realistic to look at the evolution through various life stages, rather than accepting retirement based on archaic lifestyle and age-specific transitions associated with its traditional definition. The meaning and satisfaction derived from your choices and lifestyle is more important than the timelines or methods through which you achieve fulfillment.

The financial services industry has led us to believe that the sooner we retire, the better. The financial services industry sets the bar high when it comes to the size of the ideal nest egg. Very few seniors reach this idealized goal. Human Resources administrators acknowledge the value of mature workers and express concerns about the possibility of a mass exodus of senior employees.

The impetus to encourage early retirement ebbs and flows, with growth or downturns in the economy. During buoyant economic times, employers struggle to keep mature workers and as soon as there is a downturn in the economy and they are looking to cut costs, they are quick to encourage mature workers to retire.

Renewal rather than Retirement

Billions of dollars are spent every year in North America to retard the aging process. Commercialization of age-defying products is ramping up to be the biggest growth industry. In other cultures, age is respected and viewed as the most valuable years of life.

How do we redefine ourselves and maintain our self-worth in the presence of forces that promote aging as a negative aspect of life?

What does renewal mean to you? Is it an exterior image? How about renewal from within? How about a restored interest in focusing on a life purpose? How about renewal of passion?

When our living expenses are at least partly paid by pensions, we have more opportunity to spend time differently. We have the option of investing our energy into things we value. We may choose to become activists, or to help others. These are goals that answer to our personal values. Any time we live a values driven life, we reap the reward of personal satisfaction and fulfillment.

We may explore new interests, or interests we have put on the back burner. We have more options available than any previous generation had.

CHAPTER 2

STAGES NOT AGES:

PERSONAL DEFINITION AND REALIZATION

Life is what you make it, always has been, always will be.

Grandma Moses

During the 20th Century, chronological age was a fairly accurate way of predicting the lifestyle of an individual. Typically, after completing school, most young adults got a job and married. Most people parented their first child in their early twenties. Their large families consumed their focus. Marriage and parenting dominated their lives until they were near retirement.

Then they retired. Until the last two decades, male and female roles remained distinctly different. For years the relationship between life stage and age was so closely linked that persons nearing age thirty who were still unmarried, and failed to procreate, were subjected to societal pressure. Age is no longer an indicator of life stage.

Psychologists previously designed life stage models based on finite age brackets. However, these models don't fit the majority of people born after WWII. Most of us are approaching retirement much differently than our parents, and many are leaving one job to go to another, or are exploring entrepreneurial ventures.

Some who may be financially ready are not emotionally or physically ready to terminate their relationship with their career. To pitch out the archaic social norms associated with *successful* retirement and to redesign retirement, we need strategies.

Acquiring skills to enable us to address the challenges and the impending fears or questions that plague the minds of many people nearing this life stage, will make it easier. We also need new terminology to break the cycle that leads to assumptions of what *successful* retiree lifestyles *should* look like. Existing life stage models are a good starting point for exploring how we view life transitions.

Donald Super's Theory of Vocational Stages divides career into 6 areas: Crystallization, age 14-18; Specification, age 18 – 21; Implementation, age 21 – 24; Stabilization, age 24 – 34; Consolidation, age 35 – 54; Readiness for Retirement, age 55. Boomers are seeking a healthier way of viewing retirement rather than seeing retirement as the end of the road.

The age of 65 is no longer accepted as an ideal retirement age. Many jurisdictions have passed new legislation abolishing mandatory retirement at age 65 has been passed in regions where *age 65 retirements* have been the norm for many decades. Viewing retirement as a process consisting of semi-retirement, active retirement, and bonus years is more appealing.

Pychologist Eric Erikson defined the stages of life as, various stages, assigned arbitrarily to specific age ranges, and having unique conflicts.

Oral Sensory:

- 0– 18 mo
- Trust vs. Mistrust

Muscular – Anal:

- 18 mo. - 3 yr.
- Autonomy vs. Shame/Doubt

Locomotor

- 3 - 6 years
- Purpose, Initiative vs Guilt

Independence vs Latency

- 6 - 12 years
- Industry vs. Inferiority

Adolescence

- 12 -18 years
- Identity vs. Role

Young Adulthood

- 18 - 40 years
- Isolation

Middle Adulthood

- 40 - 65 years
- Generativity vs. Stagnation

Maturity

- 65 to death
- Ego Integrity vs. Despair

According to Erikson, the adolescent identifies occupation, gender roles, politics and religion; the young adult must develop intimate relationships or suffer isolation; middle adult years focus on satisfying and supporting the next generation. Most Boomers are reaching the peak of this phase and moving into Erikson's 8th stage, *Maturity*. During Maturity, a stage described by Erikson as being age 65 to death, adults either feel a sense of fulfillment and satisfaction with their life accomplishments or they despair.

While Erikson's model identifies emotional conflicts using two emotional extremes, life is more complex than that, and a wide range of emotions may occur relating to various aspects of our lives, rather than one generalized emotion.

I met with Dr. Donald Grayston in 2008 a retired Humanities professor and Anglican priest. My intent was to discuss his transition to retirement. After retiring from his tenured position with a university, he continued to teach as a sessional instructor in a seniors' university program offering credit and non-credit courses. (Dr. Donald Grayston Born August 31, 1939 Died October 23, 2017)

His passion for Humanities, learning and instructing, played a role in the continuation of his career into his retirement. Our conversation took a philosophical direction rather than directly regarding his retirement story. Grayston shared his insight into mid-life transitions and retirement. His is perspective is worth sharing.

Dr. Grayston saw mid-life as a time when people confront their own mortality, for the first time. "They either repress their mortality or accept it and become more spiritually open. If they are still repressing their mortality at the time they move into retirement, they become depressed," he said, reminding me of Eric Erikson's Eight Stages.

Grayston used a coffee shop napkin to sketch his view of life stages as shown in Fig. 1.1. As a professor who has taught courses on Gandhi and the

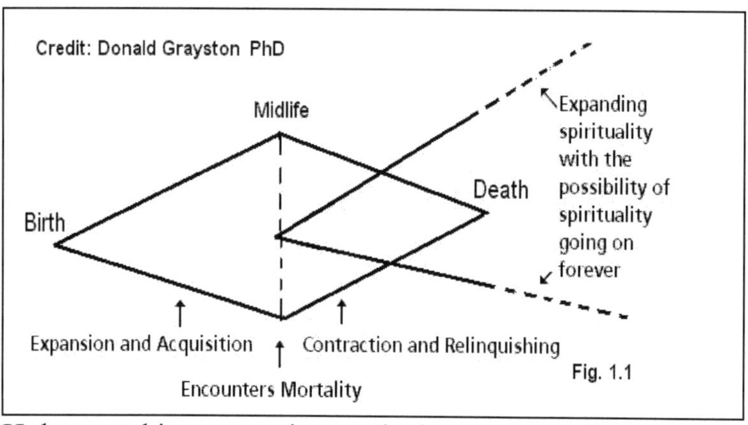

Fig. 1.1

Holocaust, his perspective on the importance of spirituality and values is not only integral to his career but also to his own life philosophy. He mentioned that Victor Frankl, in his book ***Man's Search for Meaning*** identified *sense of meaning* as being the differentiating factor between those who survived concentration camps and those who died there.

He believed it is the same in retirement. We either have a sense of meaning or purpose in life; otherwise, when confronted with challenges we lose our will to live.

The loss of purpose seems to effect health and longevity. A Human Resources manager for a company that underwent a merger resulting in a major downsizing told me that of 38 employees who were laid off, 5 had died within the first two years. Those who died were men between the ages of 48 and 52. Although health problems may have played a role in a few of these deaths, none of these men had known health issues at the time of the layoff.

Considerable research shows a correlation between people who retire early and increased early morbidity. Studies show even higher rates of early morbidity among people who have retired involuntarily 5–10 years before their expected retirement date.

In part, the shift that occurs as people relinquish their work and gravitate toward other ways of finding life meaning, may include an increased interest in spirituality.

Dr. Grayston's assertion that spirituality is the key component of successful retirement led me to query whether spirituality can be discussed as openly in the corporate sector, as it is in the academic arena.

Although he was an Anglican priest, he did not see spiritual growth and religion as synonymous, nor did he imply Christianity was the only avenue to spiritual fulfillment. He mused at how often we hear the statement: "I am spiritual, but not religious" and challenged me to see if I understood the difference.

Coffee shop napkins again entered the picture as he drew another diagram to explain his point. Spirituality may encompass religion; however, it is unnecessary for a person to be religious in order to be spiritual. It is possible to be: religious without being spiritual; religious and spiritual or spiritual and non-religious.

He explained that spirituality means many different things to different people and cultures. It is not a matter of discrediting one religious or spiritual philosophy in favor of another, but rather a matter of encouraging people to find what fits for them. How people define or express their spirituality is less important than that they reconcile their own understanding and source(s) of spiritual expression.

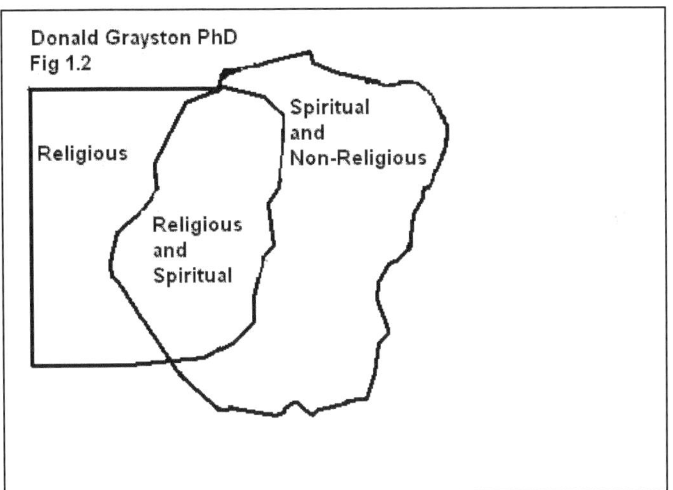

"Spirituality–life meaning and defined values–is an important component of life balance. Values are the core of spirituality. Values are relative. However, we may place greater importance on certain values in different stages of life.

For instance, when we are building a career, our values relating to contribution to society through work may rank high. While we are raising a family, family relationships may rank higher in our value system. During retirement, values may shift to placing more emphasis on giving back to the community through volunteering.

Ultimately, three or four values define and determine our identity, becoming the fundamentals of our spiritual perspective–whether religion is or is not involved. Values result from boiling down our priorities after evaluating where and why they fit in our lives. Perhaps values are the *why* that motivate us to invest our lives the way we do" Grayston explained

Even when organized religion is not part of a person's perspective of spirituality, core values seem to relate to a belief in something bigger than oneself, a higher power, God, or an afterlife. Deep factions between religious beliefs and religious differences have led to wars in every generation.

Perhaps it is the "*I'm right – you're wrong*" attitude that causes some people to reject organized religion in preference of more generic spirituality. To the pacifist it seems incomprehensible that people claiming to believe in God would war against one another–or against other people created by the same God (based on creationist theories.)

Dr. Grayston cited the 1989 fall of communism and how the communist states began, one-by-one, to abandon communism. He explained that, in many ways, institutionalized religion is heading that way–becoming more disconnected from culture, which will raise questions about the role of traditional organized religions over the next fifty years.

The US distinctly separates the church and the state. Congress does not have the right to ever determine a specific church or religion to be the official church of the country. Nevertheless, religion and politics are interconnected in the US.

The fundamentalists likely played a significant role in bringing the Bush administration to power and the church remains a stronger part of the social fabric of US culture, whereas in Canada the church is less predominantly part of the culture, and plays a smaller role in social programs.

Dr. Grayston said, "Organized religions face the challenge of offering the groundedness created by long-standing traditions without retreating to the 13th century. They need to offer traditional and contemporary meaning simultaneously. While only the most committed continue to attend church, 99% of the people in the world believe *there is something out there* while only one or two percent are agnostic or atheists–most of which are in North America or Europe.

We often associate dreams with *the other world***.** Most North Americans would say, 'I had a dream last night and my (deceased) mother was in it.' Indigenous peoples around the world for centuries have said, 'My mother came and visited me in my dream last night.' Indigenous people are implying a deceased person is returning from the afterworld to visit them during the dream state."

The whole approach to ageism, death and dying are culturally derived, not innate. Nor are they necessarily relevant to the meaning and vitality we can experience in old age. Asian cultures have taught younger generations to respect and care for the older generation. Elders in many cultures play a significant role in teaching values to children.

To a great extent North American people born in the 50s and 60s have taught their younger generation to be "me" focused, with little or no expectation of caregiving when their parents become elderly. They find themselves caught in a caregiving dilemma with elderly dependent parents and 30-year-old children living at home–sometimes divorced children returning home with a child in tow.

The extreme of the ancient Inuit custom of sending the dying on their final journey aboard an ice floe into the ocean, has met the extreme strides of medicine which enable us to prolong life. There will be no polar ice cap in another 40 years, so we won't have to worry about being sent out for a final journey on an ice floe, but the questions we must ask ourselves about aging and our rights as an aging population, need to be addressed. Individual desires need to be acknowledged.

Planning your retirement in stages to include semi-retired, active retirement and bonus years can provide clarity about your expectations at various stages of life.

Phi in the Sky

Why have 13, 21 and 55 become accepted as ages to defining our lives? The answer may surprise you. These numbers have mathematically significance. They are Fibonacci numbers. The method of applying them ignores that advances in medicine have increased longevity – yet we hold on to this system of categorizing life stages.

Phi is simply an irrational number similar to *pi*, both being mathematical numbers that repeat ad infinitum, yet seem to have strong validity in defining our world. Pi equals 3.14159265358979... *Phi* equals = 1.618033988749895... Or for the really mathematically inclined x÷1=1÷(x - 1) or x 2 – x - 1 = 0. It is just simply accepted that pi is a relevant number when calculating the circumference and diameter of a circle.

Likewise, Phi, called the *Golden Section* by Greeks and *Divine Proportion* by Renaissance artists, is accepted as a ratio of segments which is valid in nature and the universe as an explanation of proportion.

Phi is valid in the proportions of the human face and body. Proportions of other animals, plants, flowers, DNA, the solar system, population growth, and… in the stock market all demonstrate Phi. Some people believe it is the universal constant of design, the signature of God.

Phi is widely used by artists, architects, designers, engineers, musicians, photographers, sculptors, surgeons and stock market analysts to achieve excellence. If exploring how Phi works, there are many online software solutions that allow you to see for yourself.

What, you may ask, has this got to do with retirement? Intrigued by the evidence of Phi in every aspect of life, I became curious as to how Phi worked when applied against human age or life stages. I found out I wasn't the first one to think of this.

The mathematical progression developed by Phi is 1, 2, 3, 5, 8, 13, 21, 34, 55, 89. We call these Fibonacci numbers in honor of an Italian mathematician who lived between 1170 and 1250CE. Although Fibonacci gets most of the credit, this mathematical concept was used by Sanskrit or Indian scholars from as early as 400 or 250BC. It is apparent that these numbers are correlated to developmental stages and on the earlier end, our expectations of normal childhood development.

Thirteen is widely regarded as a transitional point into puberty, although girls are now entering menses younger than in previous generations. The age of 21 still remains fairly accepted as an appropriate age for legal transactions. In many states of the US, age 21 is still the legal drinking age (LDA).

In Alberta (Canada), the LDA was reduced to 18 in 1971 and during the 1980's and 1990's Alberta and other Canadian provinces raised the LDA to 19. In Italy and France LDA is only 16 and in the US, the LDA remains at 21—the highest LDA in the world.

Theories using Phi would identify 34 as the age where adult skills are fully developed and parenting roles are perceived to be in place. This too is shifting – dramatically. Age 40 is now the old age 34. Increasing numbers of people are delaying marriage and families, and careers are peaking later.

The most disturbing number is 55. This has been extensively used by the financial industry as a marker for ideal retirement and/or at least a strong indication of maximized financial net worth. It has become an age from which even those who sail through age 40 and 50 without too many emotional ripples find themselves starting to feel old. Old? 55 isn't old. Life expectancy predicts a 55 year old has about 30 years left. When you think of what a person can accomplish in 30 years, it isn't a small part of life.

The next break comes at 89 and is called "completion" stage. If viewed as ***the end*** completion seems depressing. I prefer to view it as an opportunity to apply the ***finishing touches***.

We adopt words like elderly as a label for people nearing death. This is a mistake. The word "elder" more accurately describes a person who has attained wisdom. Most aboriginal people use the word "elder" to describe a most revered person in the tribe–a person who has attained wisdom, and knowledge through life experience. Many religious groups refer to respected persons who have attained stature in the church hierarchy, as elders.

Unfortunately, Western society has abandoned the revered status of older people, opting for a flatter social structure. The downside of this is yet to be realized. It appears few teenagers today have not been taught to respect seniors. How will these impact seniors once our population swings to the place where the aging population outweighs those under 30?

A New Life Stages Model

While the life stage models of Erikson and Super provide the option of making sense of life stages, it seems they are missing one factor–flexibility. To accept age-specific stages as the ideal or to understand life stages using these models doesn't work anymore, for retirement, than it does for parenting. It is clear that we do not all fit in the same age-defined life stages.

Some Boomers have married later, parented later, or raised blended families; personal choices determine where the transitions from one life phase to another occur. This alters the reality of developmental stages; physical activity levels, shifts in parental roles and in the views and lifestyle previously labelled "retirement" call for a new life stage model.

I feel it is we need a new Life Stage Model. I created the Nielsen Life Stage Model. Various life stages overlay one another, shaping a model that fits the people – not the people needing to fit the model. Life Stages occur, but at different ages for different individuals. The model can be generalized, and applied to society. However, I believe it is more meaningful to depict the life stages of an individual to create greater understanding of one's life.

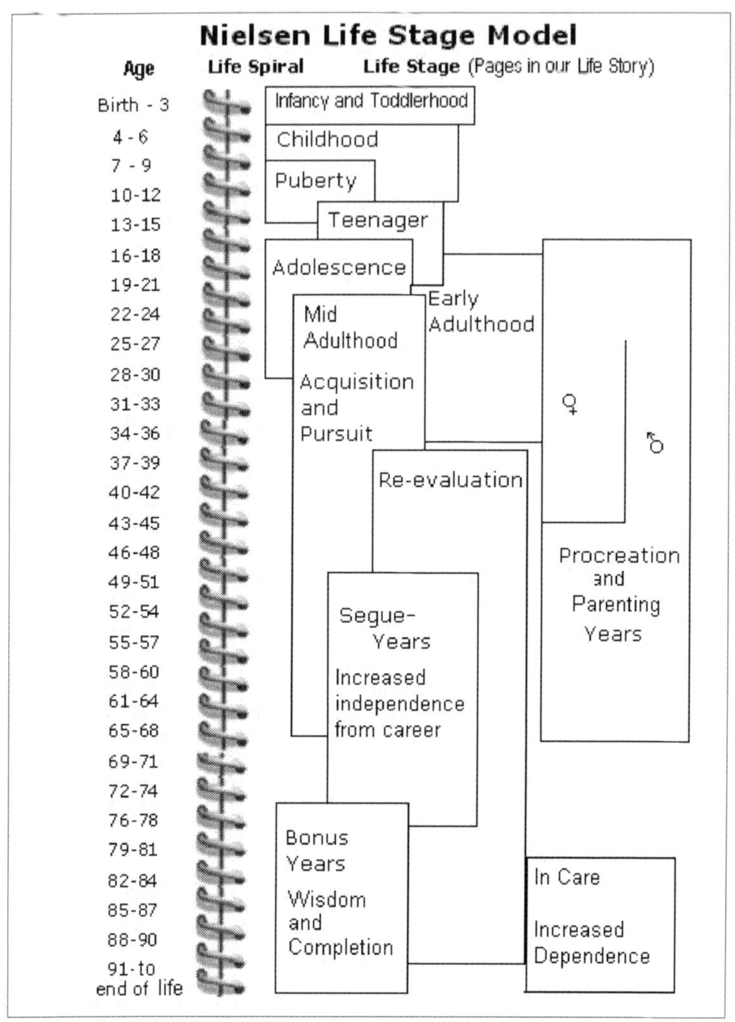

Each life stage is like a movable window moving up or down and relocated to fit the age range that suits the life of the individual. I intend it to be more fluid—recognizing that depictions of future life stages may require re-visitation as time evolves. Life stages may not always fit the same geometric shape for all people.

Definition Key for the Nielsen Life Stage Model

Infancy and Toddlerhood – Motor skill and language development, behavior patterns begin to develop. Learning through mimicry of role models.

Childhood – Early learning and behavioral development. Value system develops, influenced by role models and peers.

Puberty – Awareness of sexuality and physical development, beginning of personal identity.

Teenager – Increased assertion of personal identity, trending toward independence from parents.

Adolescence – First jobs, acceptance of responsibility for education, career and lifestyle choices and increased autonomy.

Early Adulthood – Pursuit of education and/or career advancement, seeks and achieves material and relationship goals (home, car, long-term relationships, and/or parenting). Value system and behavioral patterns stabilize. Significant other relationships and parenting may or may not occur.

Procreation and Parenting Years – Relationships include procreation and/or parenting. May occur more than once and include forming blended families. Procreation may be delayed or omitted.

Mid Adulthood: Acquisition and Pursuit – Emphasis on accomplishing material, career, educational, and relationship goals.

Re-evaluation – Value adjustments, including questioning the meaning of life, and/or priorities. Re-evaluation may lead to shift from physical acquisitions to experiential priorities; from materialism to an increased awareness of spirituality; or from individualistic to relationship and community focus.

Segue Years – Transition to increased independence from career, and reduction of acquisition-seeking activities. May include the redefinition of self, life-goals, and increased focus on life meaning.

Bonus Years (l'età dell'oro) - Wisdom and completion of life goals, mental and/or physical slowing down, relinquishing of acquisitions, departure from active community involvement and productive living to increased life of ease. Focus increasingly on closure, spirituality, fulfillment and legacy development.

In Care: Increased Dependence - Health and length of life may result in an increased need for assistance with personal care. Deteriorating physical strength and mental well-being may diminish to the point where independent self-care is no longer possible.

Stages of Life: Pages in our Life Story

The following diagram shows an example and will hopefully provide enough understanding for you to design a picture of your own life stages. Numerous life-stages may occur concurrently and the intensity of the role may increase or decrease as the life-stage unfolds.

Parenting roles and duties vary as a child matures. The intensity of the parenting role or process diminishes and may ebb out slowly or end abruptly.

Career development and completion varies from one person to another. Many leave their careers suddenly with no ongoing income-generating activity. Others leave their main career and continue some income generation through their first 5 to 20 Segue Years.

As life goals change to reflect greater time freedom and freedom from career goals, mature adults often tend toward a diminished interest in new acquisitions. Not that they will not rearrange their resources and acquisitions. Many adults at this stage sell their primary residence and move to a different city or smaller residence and/or purchase a seasonal home. Usually acquisition trends diminish in terms of possessions prior to reduction of a full-time career.

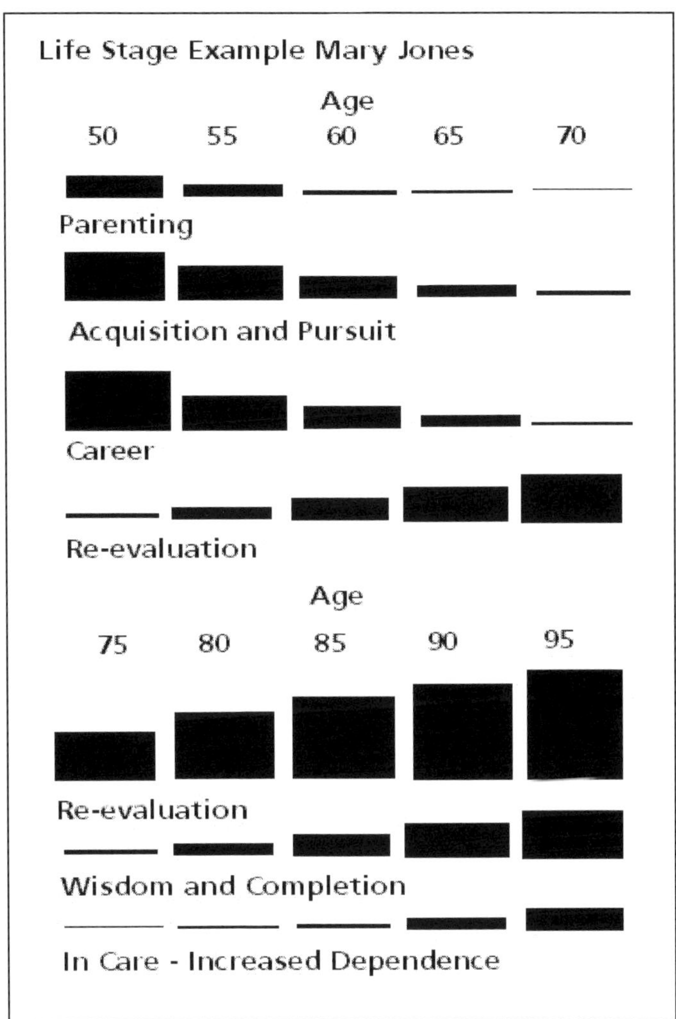

If your understanding of life is that it is the physical stage of a Spiritual experience, or if your spiritual beliefs involve an afterlife such as Heaven, then spirituality does not end with death. Death is only a transition point into another stage.

It is unnecessary to come to any agreement on the meaning of life and death; however, it will be assumed in depicting this model of life stages that there is a spiritual experience which endures death.

This assumes we adopt the forever-expanding concept of spirituality Dr. Grayston depicted in his diagram.

Depiction of life stages can be created by overlaying the life arenas that apply to the individual. The key is to understand that life stages are more relevant to your transitional process, and age expressed only as a chronological number can be irrelevant, leading to imposing unrealistic expectations on yourself.

CHAPTER 3

CONTINUAL GROWTH:
An Ongoing Process

There are no great limits to growth because there are no limits of human intelligence, imagination, and wonder.

Ronald Reagan (1911 - 2004)

The Third Age, or Troisième Age as it is called by the French, or traditional retirement in North America, tended toward withdrawal and inactivity. Today's seniors are changing this. The Segue Years are an opportunity for personal growth continuing into old age and embracing opportunities to enrich our lives, keeping us physically, mentally and spiritually young.

We all know people who seem youthful at 85 and others who seem old at 50. Numerical expression of age is inaccurate. We remain young and vital as long as we engage in the process of living and growing.

The stigma that surrounds the aging process comes from our consumer-driven society. As the number of people reaching retirement increases, advertisers bombard them with whatever they think they will buy–retirement savings plans, plastic surgery, anti-aging creams or luxury trips and leisure activities.

When we physically reach adulthood, the growth of new cells continues. Cellular regeneration continues as long as life continues. It is a process of rebirth. The renewal and replacement of the old with new cells is necessary to sustain any organism.

Lack of personal growth may not lead to physical death, but it certainly leads to stagnation. There are many people who are physically living, but are dead emotionally, spiritually and sociologically. They are existing–not living. Nature is filled with metaphors that can help us understand the process of growth and re-creation. Observing the growth cycle of the tree provides a helpful metaphorical comparison for understanding personal growth.

Pith: Letting Go

As a sapling grows, once valuable parts become dormant, and newly generated parts become active. The most central part of a tree is the pith. Pith cells are dormant and will be there as long as the tree is in existence. Pith is like our past experiences. Living in the past will zap strength needed for continued growth. Letting go of the past enables personal growth to continue.

Heartwood: Core Strength

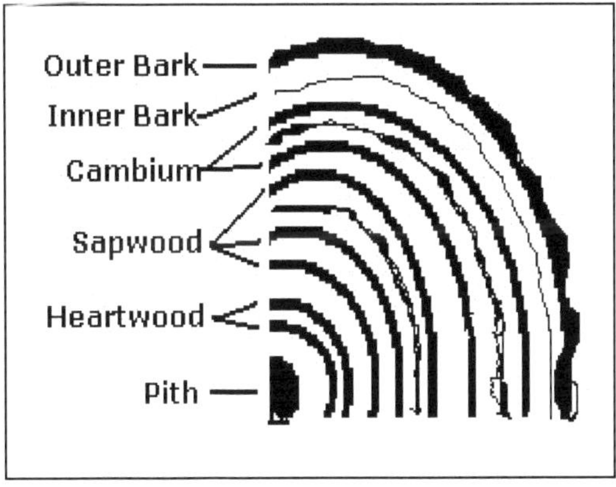

The heartwood is dead woody cells that surround the pith, making the tree trunk rigid and strong. It forms the core of the tree. The heartwood symbolizes to our earlier adult years. Life experiences build resilience and help us develop core strengths.

The heartwood allows the tree to weather storms. Just as a tree continues to grow through the drier seasons, we too grow, during the good times and during difficult times. From some of the most difficult experiences we can gather the resilience to move forward and celebrate our lives.

Developing meaningful family traditions can provide a sense of security. If these are used to celebrate and reinforce the positive aspects of the past, they can be beneficial.

Celebrating the triumphs of being at a certain stage of life and clarifying our focus enables us to have productive, rewarding lives into old age. Maturity brings with it less need to be competitive and define ourselves based on other people's expectations.

Sapwood: Nourishment for Future Growth

Next to the heartwood comes the sapwood. Sapwood is comprised of active woody cells. These cells transport water and nutrients. As new sapwood develops, the inner sapwood rings gradually become dormant to form more heartwood.

Personal growth can be stunted because of our lack of planning. Negative emotions such as guilt, remorse and resentment hinder progress. Removing these barriers is like removing a tree from a nursery pot and giving it all the room it needs to grow.

Hopefully, as we enter the Third Age, we understand that perfectionism is unachievable. Some of us have a nag inside of us, constantly telling us we are not as good as we should be. Most, if not all First Nations languages do not have a word for *should.* It is either a *want* or a *need.* Living life well requires a delicate balance between focussing our energy and becoming obsessively driven to be better and better.

Cambium Rings: Recent Growth

Next to the outer layer of the sapwood are the cambium rings. The cambium is the active growing part of the tree. Recent growth generates healthy cells, which transport and store nutrients. Well-nourished trees become stronger and more able to withstand storms with each passing year.

The day-to-day experiences of our lives provide us with nutrients for the growth and maturity to resist future storms. Without growth, decay sets in, leading to death. When the old cells are rejuvenated it enables the mature organism to continue to grow.

Inner Bark: Nurturing and Self Care

The inner bark plays a very significant role in the healthy development of the tree, by moving the food produced by the leaves, to other parts of the tree. It transports extra food to the roots, to be stored for future use.

The inner bark is symbolic of one's relationship with oneself. We must nurture ourselves and provide ourselves with nourishment - emotionally, spiritually and physically to provide for our future growth. We must be self-serving.

Outer Bark: Self Protection

The outer bark is dead. It protects the tree from fire, animals, and insects, and from damage caused by extreme temperature changes. This outer bark is like our cognitive abilities. Unlike other living organisms, we can understand abstract concepts. This can protect us from harm by our surroundings and enable us to determine our response to the environment.

Life Lessons from Nature

The tree develops earlywood in spring. When we gain a renewed understanding of how we can bring meaning to our lives, we experience a growth spurt. Latewood develops in the heat of summer. It is like the growth that takes place in our lives when we face challenging circumstances.

Fruit trees demonstrate ongoing productivity. Fruitfulness is similar to physical exercise. Exercise uses energy—but instead of reducing your energy level, it produces more energy. The more fruit we produce in our lives, the more energy we generate for future growth and the more we will have to give to others and to our community.

We can learn lessons from weeds. The dandelion can re-grow from the roots, or from seeds that mature even after the plant is destroyed. I remember my father digging a cistern when I was a child and he followed a dandelion root down to see just how long it was. To his amazement, it was more than 5 feet long. Unless the entire root was removed the dandelion could continue to grow.

Other weeds, like Morning Glory, will cling to anything. Chickweed has shallow roots but can grow from the smallest cutting. In Lower Mainland BC, one of the most tenacious weeds is the Blackberry. The barbed branches protect the berries from humans and animals that would pick all the fruit. The branches spread wildly and re-root to form new plants.

Apparently, blackberries are not indigenous to this area, yet they are tenacious and take a stronghold even in cities. It provides a metaphor for a life lived in an unhealthy environment, causing us to become like the barbed plant–seeking self-protection and in the process becoming an annoyance to others.

We determine the type and quality of fruit we will produce when we develop our vision. Grafting fascinated my father. He would graft a branch from one kind of fruit tree into another, to take advantage of the strengths of both species. We can graft things into our personal plan that will enable us to be more productive, using our strengths and benefiting from the strengths of others.

We can attract experiences into our lives that enhance our growth potential. Continuing to enjoy life is dependent on our ability to recognize cycles, embrace them and take from each stage the lessons learned, and apply them to the future.

Just think of some acquaintance who is a real joy to be around, and I will bet it won't be a person who is just allowing life to happen. Successfully living a fulfilling life is not the result of a weed patch of random acts; it is a well-tended planned landscape and garden.

CHAPTER 4

AGE 65 PARADOX:

A POWERFUL GENERATION

I have enjoyed greatly the second blooming.. suddenly you find – at the age of 50, say – that a whole new life has opened before you.

Agatha Christie (1890 – 1976)

The decision of when to retire can be complex. In organizations where pensions enable earlier departures from work, the lure of maxing out pensions often takes precedence over job satisfaction. Employees who are not eligible for company pensions often work past 65, motivated by financial need or job satisfaction.

The *pension trap* is not as significant as people may think—it is best to consult your financial planner to explore options. The demise of compulsory retirement at age 65 may result in some of the least capable people feeling they need to continue working well beyond age 65. Deteriorating health may be a factor in decisions. Many people start encountering health problems as they approach their 70's, if not sooner, and it is possible for all of their healthy years to have been invested in working, with little time to experience travel and active health while enjoying freedom from full-time career commitments.

For low-income employees, who are often women, the option of retiring and relying on government pensions can present an even more difficult decision. Will the removal of age 65 retirement alter eligibility for some of the benefits previously available?

Taking a reduced earlier pension can have advantages. Ron, an engineer working for a municipal government, plans to take a reduced pension at age 50 and accept a job in the private sector–a job that will pay two times as much as his present job. This is a financially beneficial move if he invests his pensions.

Another gain for Ron will be job satisfaction. He states he is stifled by bureaucracy at his present job and looks forward to new opportunities and challenges. Ron expects he will work to age 65, however he finds it difficult to understand people who are interested in working past that age.

Carol is second in command in a major US government department in Washington, DC. She has five years left to max out her pensions. She has loved her job and was making great progress in implementing changes that would vastly improve the lives of 2 million Americans every year. For Carol, the prospect of having the ability to improve the lives of so many people filled her with passion. Then, a new commissioner was appointed, and everything changed. Now, Carol faces many tough decisions.

It seems the impact she felt so confident about making will not happen. To stay in this position means instead of ending on a high note, it is more likely to end with feelings of frustration and maybe even failure. She could take early pensions and leave now–avoiding increased frustration. An opportunity in Baltimore holds the promise of ending her career on a high note.

She has done the math. If she takes her pension early and invests the earnings while continuing to work elsewhere during the next five years, she can come out ahead of the game financially. However, it means a 2-hour daily commute. Factors influencing her decision include: Should her husband retire first? Will they continue living in DC as long as they continue to work? Will changing jobs make her feel like a quitter? Do they need to make a decision *now* as to which state they want to live in during retirement?

She has no concerns about a social network. She has no financial concerns. Her greatest fear is how their marriage of 35 years will fair through retirement. They have a great marriage, she says, however – the marriage works because work-related travel gives them independence. The transition to retirement could result in non-stop availability to share schedules and be together too much.

This is a situation many people find themselves in as they step away from their careers. There are strong arguments for making your last five years the high point in your career. When frustrations with management or organizational changes thwart one's expectations, it can be better to change jobs.

After 3 months of careful contemplation, Carol and her husband made some decisions: Carol will remain in her position for another 6 months before making her final decision. Right now there are a few changes pending that will clarify the direction of her department. Should the outcome escalate Carol's frustrations, she will move to another job.

It won't be a job in Baltimore. She will pursue a job in the community where they intend to retire. A flexible work schedule for her and the option of telecommuting for her husband are priorities. Carol mentioned she is beginning to worry about financial security. As for many people, the unknowns such as illness and the cost of maintaining the lifestyle to which they are accustomed leaves serious questions as to how much money is enough. Carol admits that most of her interests are costly and inappropriate for a couple existing on a fixed income.

Carol has many hobbies and interests, and both she and her husband are eager to travel and take university-level courses as a replacement for their career commitments. It seems that Carol has already made her choice and that the 6 month wait is only a formality to be sure she is not making rash decisions. Realistically, 6 months is not too long to wait when making a life change of this magnitude.

In some relationships, the husband and wife are equals; in other situations clearly one has more power than the other. Decisions during the transition have a huge impact on marital relationships. Most marriages go through a rough spot when each spouse leaves their career. This can happen twice if one leaves work sooner than the other; it can also be very difficult if both spouses leave full-time careers at the same time.

Unhealthy marriages may become healthier during retirement; For some marriages, the shift from career to retirement can be the demise of the relationship. Often, good marriages rebound to be better than ever during The Segue Years.

Never too Young to Retire

What is the ideal age to segue? In 2006, the average age of the first retirement in the US was about 62 years—often followed by a return to at least, part-time work.

Between 1976 and 2000, Canada's average retirement age fell from 65 to an all-time low of 61.5, where it hovered for a decade.

In Canada, the average retirement age increased by 2 years from a decade earlier. Average public sector retirement age was 62, private sector employee age 64 and the self-employed retirement age was on average 67.

In Canada, in 2018, the number of people aged 100 and older grew by 41.3 per cent from a decade earlier.

It remains to be seen how increased longevity will affect retirement age. The question is do people work longer because their health allows it, or do they work longer because they fear they will run out of money?

Many people are able to retire earlier if they have good pensions from work, have had a stable life with few if any interruptions such as lay-offs, divorce or illness and if they have been wise and successful investors. This, unfortunately, is a relatively small percentage of the overall population.

If you have apprehensions about your finances during the Segue Years you are far from alone— that may not mean you can't retire younger. Increasing numbers of segue-aged employees are choosing to abandon their primary career and transition to a more independent lifestyle–either through a career change, a transition to part-time work, or through self-employment. While these options are in some respects retirement, the definition must stretch like bubble gum to encompass this transition.

An ongoing transitional process becomes a more effective way to describe this trend. Although it is necessary to discuss retirement at times, using the traditional meanings of retirement, let's take a few moments to redefine retirement. We can remove the age expectation and show the appeal of renaming and redefining retirement.

Today's seniors are painting a much more positive picture than the old retirement. Segue Years are:

- ongoing life transitions, moving mature adults through chosen changes toward a life of their dreams

- the most ideal state of adult development, where *becoming* is less important and *being* is emphasized

- a desirable life status, where leisure, physical activity, social interconnectedness, relationships and financial balance allow the individual to enjoy time freedom and self-expression

- a life stage where the individual can be self-directed and participate in activities and/or lifestyle not possible earlier in life

- a career stage where the individual merges livelihood with life purpose, achieving balance and security

Segue Years are an era of life that shifts in many life arenas including:

- **Career:** income generation, career transition, succession or completion, reduced engagement, the shift from corporate to entrepreneurial ventures

- **Community:** social activism; revival of interest in community and relationships, activation and realization of personal dreams

- **Life Balance:** social, psychological, physical, financial and spiritual well-being; productivity, creation and recreation; merging of work with fun or life purpose; launching and operating an entrepreneurial venture that enables time freedom

- **Self Care and Reflection:** caring for health, travel, legacy creation, exploration of life meaning

From this vantage point, there is no such thing as being too young to segue, nor is there an ideal age to start your *Inspirement*. Work fulfils an important role in people's lives. Some people enjoy the structure of a 9 to 5 job and routine work. The solutions are as diverse as people are individuals.

Based on a broader, more joyous view of retirement, the options become liberating, and gathering the information you need to make choices that are right for you is increasingly interesting and important. Making the choice to enter your Segue

Years is based on redesigning your life to bring greater satisfaction, sooner appears to be better than later.

The financial industry has overworked retirement as a tool for generating sales, to most adults making little preparation for retirement other than attempting to save money. Those who have not succeeded in setting aside the Retirement Nest Egg the financial industry tells them they need, feel a sense of panic as they near 65.

Unfortunately, statistics show that despite the constant barrage of advertising by the financial industry, only a few have the financial resources in place for 30–45 years of leisure living. Then along came the skin care companies, dermatologists and plastic surgeons to bump up the negativity around the aging process to an all-time high.

In a society where so many companies use any excuse to capitalize on people's fears, this type of hype is as harmful as the skin-and-bone images of young models. It is interesting that there is so much pressure to change the attitude toward skinny models because of anorexia in teens and young women – yet another marketing craze, just as psychologically damaging is directed at older women, rolls ahead full steam.

An honest look at the ageing process shows that it isn't all beautiful–but at what stage is life always beautiful? The human experience contains ugliness and beauty at all times. Accidents, sickness, and crises of all types occur at any age–not just to retirees.

Statistically, illness and disease increase with age – even though there is an abundance of healthful living choices a person can make to reduce the speed of the aging process and drastically reduce the likelihood of disease.

Billions of dollars go to cancer cures. Yet far too few people focus on their ability to play a role in prevention. We need a switch in our thinking from a medical model of health – where you wait until you get sick and go in search for a cure – to an alternative health model that looks for ways to slow the ageing process and reduce risk factors.

Perhaps it is our individual perspective on the aging process that determines the point at which our life begins to deteriorate. Negativity toward the aging process is like packing your suitcase now for a trip you may take sometime in the next five years. Dove™ is leading the way with older models, promoting acceptance of wrinkles and sagging skin–providing us with greater opportunities for self-acceptance.

Humans are living longer, are more capable of being contributing members of society, and are physically active far longer than previous generations. There are stories of people well into their 80s and 90s that would put to shame lots of people in their 40s or 50s.

Otto von Bismarck was the German Chancellor who led the way for Germany to become the first country in the world to adopt an old-age, social insurance program in 1889. The idea was for the state to provide for people who, because of age or invalid state, could not provide for themselves. Bismarck believed this would generate well-being among workers and that it would benefit the economy and silence calls for more socialist alternatives.

Bismarck chose age 70, when the average life expectancy of Germans was only 72. To extrapolate a ratio based on today's life expectancy, pensions would begin at about 84. While life expectancy has increased, retirement age has remained steady around age 65–an age change adopted by Germany in 1916 and by the Americas as social security programs came into being in the US and Canada.

The message has been to save enough money prior to 65 to retire and live a life of leisure—or you are a failure. It is time we change how we view retirement and how we measure success. If financial wherewithal is the only measure of success, that leaves more than half the population of North America in a no-win situation. Live life well—right now—no matter what age you are.

Simple changes can make a big difference. For example, if you value family relationships, it is better to sit on a blanket in a park sharing a meal together, than sharing the same meal while moping in front of a TV and lamenting your misfortune…or not communicating at all. You can live a life of freedom by sorting out your priorities and aligning yourself and your lifestyle with your life purpose.

You can live the life of your dreams–sooner than you think.

Is Retirement Hazardous to Your Health?

For some retirees, these will be the happiest days of their lives, for others the picture is not so rosy. Statisticians and our culture loosely refer to retirement as the time one leaves their career. Some transition in their 50s. Others wait until they are in their 60s or beyond. Regardless of the age, most men and women go through a major transition—most often including a redefinition of their career.

More than ever people are designing a lifestyle that is uniquely their own–to match their needs, interests and financial means. What are some challenges that impact their ability to segue with ease and what are some solutions to the challenges they face?

In 2018, 25% of Canadians aged 15 and older said that, in the past year, they had cared for or helped someone who had a long-term health condition, a physical or mental disability, or problems related to aging. Support Received by Caregivers in Canada, by Darcy Hango. Many adults over age 50 are caring at least part-time for aging parents. The *Sandwich Generation* refers to those who have dependent or semi-dependent children on one side and aging parents becoming increasingly dependent on the other side.

In the US, the situation is similar:

Caregivers caring for cancer, dementia, stroke patients or other long-term illness patients frequently experience depression. Scholarly articles show higher levels of depression among female caregivers. Oliver Riedel, PhD; et al in the Overlooking Informal Dementia Caregivers' Burden stated “Overall, 73.7% of caregivers had at least one somatic condition and 43.7% had clinically relevant depressive symptoms (of these, 37.5% met criteria for major depression)” (Research in Gerontological Nursing. 2016;9(4):167-174)

More than 133 million Americans, or 45 percent of the population, have at least one chronic condition. Of these, 41 million were limited in their daily activities. (Source: Tackling the burden of chronic diseases in the USA. Lancet 2009;373(9659):185)

Elderly caregivers with a history of chronic illness themselves, and who are experiencing caregiving related stress, have a 63% higher mortality rate than their non-caregiving peers.

According to Families Caring for an Aging America, (2016) Approximately 77% of home care services are provided by family caregivers.

As some people reach retirement, they find themselves caregiving for children born to them later in life, and children from a blended family. The age at which children are leaving home has increased. In 1981 only 41% of children between 20 and 24 were living at home, according to Statistics Canada, By 2016 62.6% in of children between 20 and 24 were living with parents. 70,000 Canadian grandparents are raising grandchildren.

In the US, the percentage of young adults living with parents or grandparents is much lower. Pew Research Center, found that 33% of 25-29-year-olds lived with their parents or grandparents in 2016. This is almost three times as many as in 1970. It is also the highest percentage in 75 years.

This doesn't mean continued happiness is unachievable as we age. Psychologists have provided years of research verifying that happiness has more to do with attitude than it has to do with circumstances. Making a conscious choice to take the steps to ward off depression must be a priority. The stats relating to serious depression among retirees are staggering. This may sound like retirement is dangerous and unappealing.

The key to happy Segue Years is purposeful living and learning attitudes that generate peace and happiness. People often spend more time planning for a two-week vacation than they do for 20 or 30 years of life after work. Retirement planning must include more than financial planning. Retirement expert Dr. Richard Johnson, PhD says we must find a replacement for the five benefits work has provided.

He identifies these as: financial compensation, time management, a sense of utility, status, and socialization. Dr. Johnson has designed a scientifically valid assessment instrument, the Retirement Success Profile, to assess retirement-readiness. When administered by a qualified Retirement Coach, the tool can prove beneficial to the client.

Equally important is developing a personal understanding of what will bring meaning to you. A gradual reduction of commitment to work or working part-time, volunteering, mentoring, and developing other activities that provide meaning and purpose are a large part of a happy transition. According to Dermot O'Reilly et al (Volunteering and Mortality Risk 2017) Volunteers have a lower mortality rate, at respective ages, than non-volunteers with lifestyles that were otherwise similar.

In the US a longitudinal study by Shan P Tsai from 1973 to 2003 (Age at retirement and long term survival of an industrial population) compared men and women who retired at ages 55, 60, and 65: "Mortality rates improve with an older retirement age. The study included 839 employees who retired at age 55 and 1,929 employees who worked until age 60 and who were still alive at age 65.

Overall, 137 workers who retired by age 55 died by age 65, while only 98 workers who retired at age 60 died by age 65. After adjusting for gender and socioeconomic status, the research concluded that people who retired at age 55 had almost double the mortality risk of those who continued to work into their 60s." Shan P. Tsai, et al.

Research shows continued contribution, through continued work or volunteering, adds to vitality and longevity. While it isn't clear whether health at the time of earlier retirement plays a role, numerous studies seem to indicate that there is a correlation between involuntary retirement and retirement by choice.

There is increasing evidence that our perspectives and response toward circumstances play a larger role in longevity than do the circumstances themselves. Definitely, our ability to cope successfully with life challenges increases our ability to enjoy life.

An attitude of gratitude and a zest for life are two common denominators that permeate the lives of people who have lived past 100. If you are a young grump, you will become an old grump and if you want to live longer, staying positive may play a larger role than you realize. A positive attitude improves quality of life, at any age.

Using an Action Plan increases the successful completion of goals. As with financial planning, starting early is most advantageous. Developing a plan can change your post-work life from ho-hum to a revitalizing experience, filled with opportunities to celebrate your individuality and a time to enjoy the best years of your life.

CHAPTER 5

RETHINKING THE WORKPLACE:

THE MEANING OF WORK

I never feel age...If you have creative work, you don't have age or time.

Louise Nevelson (1900 - 1988)

When the economy is in a downturn, employers hope more employees will retire. They offer voluntary severance packages and outplacement counseling. When the economy is vibrant, employers scramble to retain employees. Employers view retirement seminars and coaching as a way of increasing re-engagement among those nearing retirement who are still valuable to the employer.

However, retirement coaching and seminars also play a role in relieving stress for employees preoccupied with the complexity of retirement decisions, by increased dialogue between HR departments and employees.

If employees are facing internal turmoil about the retirement process, they may be less engaged in their job on a day-to-day basis. With the removal of mandatory age 65 retirement, employers are looking for ways to deal with employees who have *quit without leaving.*

Coaching can help the employee feel more focused on a personal career time-line. When a person within five years of retirement re-evaluates the work—he or she may experience a re-engagement with work, as they come to recognize that the benefits achieved through work exceed mere financial benefits.

Coaching and seminars increase morale—not only among older employees but throughout the entire workforce. It generates good will as the employees see their employer as supportive of their employees at all life stages. Part of a healthy retirement process involves replacing the sense of community, psychological well-being, and sense of identity achieved through work.

Employees who engage in personal development become more effective in the workplace. People who are seeking to be the best they can be in various aspects of life are the same people who have a desire to be the best they can be in their present position.

Not all employees want to quit working at 55, 60 or even 65. For increasing numbers, there is an attraction to staying involved. They want to continue working—full-time or part-time. Many are changing to new careers that allow them to merge their interests and transferable skills from their primary career.

As the responsibility of saving for retirement shifts from the employer to the employee, employer engagement in supporting the transition becomes more important. The messages employers send to their employees, by offering retirement coaching as they reach the last 5 years, can increase loyalty to the company.

What are Employers Thinking?

Some employers worry about the wave of employees that will depart over the next ten years.

Few employers have changed the structure of the workplace to adapt to employees who want in a gradual transition from full-time work to reduced hours. Corporations with large percentages of senior employees are struggling to do Succession Planning—planning to transfer knowledge that could leave with long-term employees and planning to absorb the financial ramifications of hiring and training new employees. For the most part, employers are not prepared—many have their heads in the sand.

I interviewed numerous HR Managers. I asked them how they felt the baby-boomer bubble was going to affect work the workplace. They were willing to share general information, but asked to remain anonymous.

At a recent Succession Planning workshop, employers expressed their concerns. A municipal HR manager reported, "Based on the age of the organization itself and the longevity of employees within the organization, we are facing huge issues with succession planning. Thirty percent of our workforce are 60-year-olds or better. By 2020, fifty percent will be eligible to retire. As we are a large organization, we are less able to be flexible about gradual retirement arrangements or employees coming back to help with specific projects."

Anita, a HR Manager from a company employing 140 people, expressed that “the ability for the company to bring people back on contract or on an occasional part-time basis can bridge the gap for individuals who themselves are facing financial stresses in retirement. Employees from smaller companies sometimes face a greater challenge financially than retirees from organizations where pensions exist.”

A HR Manager from a university stated, “I don’t think it is reasonable at all for employees to expect their employer to adapt the workplace environment to their changing personal needs.” The university employs many new people on a part-time or temporary basis; They prefer to hire new people for these positions as opposed to transitioning full-time tenured people into part-time, term or temp positions. Some professors have returned as sessional faculty—at a much lower rate of pay.

Donna, a HR administrator at another university, reminds us that in academia, the hiring practices are fairly decentralized. While HR gathers the resumes, then hands them to the various faculties for interviews and hiring. This has two interesting implications: First, it makes it more difficult to gauge age of new hires or people with disabilities. Second, universities develop overall guidelines and policies in order for HR to have some control over human resources in the organization—beyond that it is the decision of the department.

Unionized organizations seem most inflexible. Concern about benefits, seniority and the quandary of setting precedents can complicate issues surrounding other forms of leave including illness leave, parental leave and roles of employer-employee relationships. While organizations cannot enforce mandatory retirement, they can refuse employees the option of job sharing or the transition from full-time to part-time work.

Even an organization named *Best Employer of the Year* demonstrated that their rules around the retirement process are inflexible. Organizations with pension plans usually offer early retirement at a combined total of 80 or 85 (combined years of service plus age). Some employers reported 2/3 of employees leave as soon as they reach the magic number for pension eligibility.

However, at another organization, the HR representative stated, "Although many of our employees are eligible for retirement, an increasing number are staying as long as they can—often up to five or more years. We have been allowing people to return on contract after they retire, based on pension eligibility, to facilitate the start of pension payments combined with continued income generation. Usually pension funds are capped, disallowing people any ability to contribute to pensions after they have reached 65 or whatever the magic number." Seemingly, this shows job satisfaction plays a role in the decision to leave, and pension eligibility is not the sole reason for leaving.

Many major government organizations, major utility companies, and similar organizations where long-term employment has been the norm are now facing a tidal wave of people eligible or nearly eligible for retirement. In one city, when I asked employers how many of their employees are eligible for retirement within five years, they told me:

- major university - 42%
- major utility supplier - 55%
- municipal office - 48%

This totaled just over 1400 employees. The concern of all these employers is succession planning. Often people give little or no notice of their intention to leave.

Wake-Up Call

Many companies are lulling themselves into complacency, assuming that the mass exodus of their most senior and qualified employees, from the workforce won't affect them. Nothing could be further from the truth. If over the next five years, an organization down the street has 400 employees (or 30% of their workforce) leave, where do they suppose the replacements will come from? The ability of employees to pick where they will and won't work and their pay may spark inflation and bankruptcies in companies that can't remain competitive, causing a dramatic economic shift that even economists can't accurately predict.

Melissa, a young HR administrator, has a theory why companies are so slow to make the preparations they need to make for the exodus of senior employees: "The Baby Boomer executives will not be willing to relinquish their control to the next generation: they will stay as long as they can—even if that thwarts the company's growth. They want the company to run in a certain way and aren't as open to change as they may need to be. The Boomer exodus will create a dramatic ripple effect. Younger employees are behind the maturity curve of people the same age a decade ago. We find many young people remaining at home while they go to university, and as a result, they have a difficult time with their first job. Unless young people have moved out and traveled, they just don't have the life experience that translates into maturity."

"Employee engagement is an issue that relates to any age," says Teresa, HR manager in a large environmental firm. "We have considerable employee engagement problems with people who have been with the company for five to ten years. They will buy into what we are doing as we are on the cutting edge of technology to stop global warming. It is a politically hot topic and most employees are keen to buy into the vision. However, the question is, do they have respect for the company, respect for decisions made by management and respect for other employees? Often they don't."

She cited, "This often evolves from discontentment over a few promotions they expected or projects that didn't go where they expected they would go. They become somewhat cynical. About half the time when this happens the employee will make a choice to leave the company. Other times they will stay and be discontent with their job and cause a lot of problems. It becomes very hard work to re-engage these employees. Putting them through a battery of tests to isolate the contributing factors may offer insight into the problem."

At the very least, all companies need to look at what employees want—job satisfaction. Aside from financial considerations, the top three criteria for job satisfaction are:

- Time flexibility—including telecommuting, flexible time off or job sharing
- Working conditions—including management and co-worker relationships
- Recognition for contribution—external and internal rewards relating to the work done

Response to change is challenging for individuals. It is even more challenging for large corporations. The larger the organization, the more difficult it is for them to adapt their policies and procedures to meet the changing needs of individuals or demographic groups, such as the Plus 50 demographic. Large government organizations, universities, and international corporations are most unable to adapt quickly to changing needs of their employee demographics. The more autonomous the decision-making powers of the individual departments, the less capable the HR department becomes to implement changes to accommodate mature-to-retirement transitions for the employees.

Most retirement coaches who work with organizations are not sending a message of 'retire; the sooner the better'. Coaches seek to identify how you can get the most fulfilment out of your life–

including your career. Work fulfils an important function and recognizing the benefits of work and aligning that to your personal expectations, on and off the job, are an important factor for both the employee and the employer. Employers benefit from employees who want to be there; not from employees who feel they have no choice but to show up for work.

Employers who allow gradual transitions to retirement and who explore options for job-sharing and flexible time off will fare better as the mass exodus of Boomers occurs. Just because they predict that many will continue to work full or part-time after they turn 55 or even 65, it is no indication that they will stay with their primary career or current employers.

Some employers are definitely leading the way, recognizing well in advancc thc importancc of supporting their older workers. They recognize their contribution to the workplace and are open to dialogue and coaching programs that address the needs of workers as they age.

Working the Segue Years

When choosing to go elsewhere, most often the difference older employees are seeking is a less stressful type of job, offering greater flexibility–particularly time flexibility. For some people, retirement may provide the opportunity to do something quite different from one's traditional career.

Mature workers in transition express an unwillingness to work in inflexible, stressful, high-pressure work environments. Tracy went from an Admin Support staff position at a college to working part-time as a receptionist in a hair salon. The perks included free salon services and a low-stress, enjoyable job meeting people.

Aside from the customer service sector—a sector that for many mature employees holds less appeal—seeking opportunities that allow the ability to contract services seems to offer the best fit and recognition for past accomplishments. As employees approach 60, more and more, are looking for opportunities to merge their lifestyle and their income generation. They are more motivated to design an entrepreneurial opportunity to fit their interests and skills.

The career-related choices of the Plus 50 demographic are the beginning of a massive social shift. Employers interviewed showed that more employees are staying longer than the employees predicted five years ago, and many retirees will change jobs at least once during the next decade. Eighty percent of pre-retirees expect to work in some capacity past age 65. Although cost of living, lack of retirement savings and absence of company pension plans have led to this shift, often the decision comes because of fear of escalating medical and long-term care expenses, inflation, loss of security and inability to manage on government pensions.

Positive social change cannot come from complacency. It comes from a person or groups of people who have a vested interest in the change. If this generation wishes to change outmoded definitions of aging and retirement, the onus rests on their shoulders. Governments are responders, not initiators, and are slower than grass-roots movements in instituting change. Government's attempt to implement the desires of their constituents; until the public makes their wants known—there is nothing to act upon.

Generational shifts are clear in every facet of life. Each generation feels the ripples of change from the generations before and after them. Ironically, by the time the oldest generation is least able to self-advocate for their needs, the next generation is holding the decision-making power. Even though we like to think of ourselves as more enlightened and socially aware, the generation gap continues and manifests in every aspect of life.

David, a HR Manager, explained a new challenge facing older store managers supervising Generation "X" and Generation "Y" employees. The younger generations often consider text messaging as an acceptable replacement for face-to-face social interaction—a far cry from what Boomers were doing for social interaction when they were between 17 – 25 years of age. Text messaging is an increasing problem for some employers—a probable advantage for the mature worker who is seeking to compete in the job market.

Another interesting trend David mentioned is what he calls "Helicopter Parents" (a term first used by school teachers in the early 90s)—usually mothers who had children later in life. They land on the managers or Human Resources departments in defense of their children—even when the children are 22 – 25 years of age.

Perhaps this reflects the number of young adults still living at home. More parents hover over their children. These children are still living at home, attending university or working full time. They are overly protective. In the late 1960s and 70s kids over 20-years-of-age were called "*late bloomers*" (a derogatory term) if they were still living at home.

The employer's challenge is that the employment contract is between the adult child and the company, not the parents and the company. However, as the company's target market fits the demographic of the parents, diplomacy is a must. In an age when blogs and internet forums can quickly spread bad press, it is paramount to be tactful.

When parents get involved, David clarifies that the relationship is between the employee and the employer and not between the parent and the employer, and then states that due to privacy laws he cannot discuss it with them.

Generation "Y's" (born 1970-1990) have a strong solidarity through their massive network of text messaging friends and have the potential of influencing many of their peers based on their opinions and the ability to spread messages quickly.

Perhaps the challenge for Boomers is the diverse expectations and needs they have. Many of the resources early retirees will need to meet their challenges are not available. Will social support and government programs be there when needed? To what extent does the onus rest on the Plus 50 demographic to initiate social change? Will it come from grassroots efforts or will it depend on solidarity?

As Margaret Mead stated, “A small group of thoughtful people could change the world. Indeed, it’s the only thing that ever has.” Before we can actively initiate a shift on a societal level, we need to be clear about what we want as individuals. Initiating change in a culture begins at the individual level. Just as the Boomer population initiated shifts of cultural norms in their youth, they are likely to bring another wave of change as they move through the last half of their lives. Many become social activists for causes they believe in, after they stop working.

Shattering the Silver Ceiling

Ageism is widespread, and the pains it evokes are about to reach tsunami proportions over the next two decades unless we take action to redefine aging and retirement. Barriers to employment and advancement in the workforce have changed over the decades.

In the 1980s, they often faced these barriers because of race or gender. In the March 24, 1986 edition of the Wall Street Journal, Carol Hymowitz and Timothy Schellhardt introduced the term *Glass Ceiling*. Since then, Glass Ceiling has become a widely accepted term referring to promotions denied based on gender or race.

Now there is apparently a similar hurdle, raising questions about employment equality for the mature adult—the *Silver Ceiling* - which seems to cut right through the hair dye. Ask most people over 45 and in a forced career transition, if there is a *Silver Ceiling* and there will be a resounding "yes!"

Ageism is a human rights issue and can land a company in a lawsuit. Ageism may stem from a supervisor who feels intimidated about supervising someone who is their elder, or an employer who makes a premature judgment of the mature worker's likelihood of being able to do the job or fit into a new corporate culture.

Companies with a marginal number of older employees seem to be the most resistant to hiring retired people who wish to reenter the workforce. Having a lower-aged demographic in their workforce seems to correlate with doubting the productivity of older employees. Ironically, just as many employers voiced serious dissatisfaction with employees under 30, citing them as less loyal, with a poorer work ethic, prone to take days off to ski and managing their social life via email, text messaging or cell phone during work hours.

Age is not the main determinant of employee effectiveness and if another applicant's education seems more up-to-date and relevant to the needs of the employer, it can put the mature applicant at a disadvantage. A few years ago, Martin attended an interesting job interview, where candidates were interviewed in a group.

The company was young and dynamic–the average age of employees was about 28. Martin was definitely qualified to be a Marketing Manager. Against the 5 other candidates, he felt considerably more experienced.

Martin was, however, 60 years old, and most of the other applicants were twenty-something, newly graduated MBA's. Could he do the job? Yes, although he would face a considerable challenge to adapt to their highly computerized environment. Although Martin had worked on computers, he was slower when using a computer. In a fast-paced computerized environment, he was not perceived as their ideal fit. Martin found it difficult to compete with younger job applicants. Martin decided he needed to start a business of his own.

Maturity can work in favor of the person with a great attitude. However, for the person who has become cynical, finding a new job—or satisfaction in an existing job—becomes increasingly questionable. Some mature workers who seem to have difficulty reintegrating themselves into the workforce, usually have anger management problems, or other attitudinal problems that show up during job interviews.

Employees who do not exhibit a willingness to be self-monitoring and team players earlier in their careers have escalating problems that become barriers to employment as they age. This appears to be a common sentiment among employers.

There are many companies and opportunities where age is an advantage, leading to employers who seek mature workers. A HR Manager in a ten-year-old medium-sized technical company stated that, “We appreciate the opportunity to hire mature workers. They may not be as technically up-to-date, however they make up for this in maturity, adaptability to change and are typically lower maintenance than younger employees.”

An openness, or even preference toward hiring mature workers is obvious in companies where interaction with the public, customer service or handling of cash was part of the job description, versus more professional or technical positions.

These companies describe mature new-hires using words such as: dependable, low-maintenance, self-directed, cooperative, and even-tempered. They often described younger workers as career-driven, quick, willing to deal with pressure, eager to learn. The shift in language used to describe qualities in younger, and mature employees seems to reoccur in interviews with HR administrators often enough to question whether stereotyping occurs even if it is not intentional.

As employers seek those employees who fit their corporate culture, mature workers likewise need to seek companies that fit them. Job interviews are always sales opportunities. You are there to sell the organization on why they should hire you. Understanding how to sell your skills by understanding their needs and by emphasizing the strengths of yourself as a mature employee goes a long way in opening doors.

It is those who most often have the higher-paying jobs that are less prone to quit working earlier. The higher the level of education, the more likely a person is to maintain their career as long as they can. Less educated employees face a double dilemma; they are less able to find alternative employment, often cannot stash away retirement savings and are less appealing to employers, as many HR departments favor education over experience.

A dilemma arises from a desire to reduce one's working life from full-time to part time. Often the employee who wants to engage in a gradual reduction of hours finds that if their employer is not open to this arrangement, they have to either stay or risk difficulty finding a new employer.

The larger the bureaucracy, the less likely the employer is to engage in job-sharing. This creates a sense of powerlessness by employees. They feel the security is too difficult to leave. This can be a real trap. The question an employee has to ask is, "What do I really want?"

The sense of having no choice is very detrimental to a person's well-being. We often become so close to our situation that we can't visualize anything different. The fact is—anything is possible. It depends on how deep your desire is. There are always more choices than we can see.

Although employers have a responsibility to accommodate disabled employees, there seems to be a gap between that responsibility and understanding the needs of people as health issues alter their ability to do their job. Often, health issues come gradually with age and the employer is often unwilling to see the adaptation of the work environment as the employer's responsibility.

Many employers express doubt they would offer an employee an opportunity to move to a less demanding job within the company—citing they would question the employee's ability to feel fulfilled in what the employee may perceive as a demotion. This can lead to people leaving and later finding themselves looking for work with another employer.

While a survey of employers verifies that the workforce is age-diverse, there are some industries where the age demographic is skewed. Technology-related businesses, particularly younger companies, have a lower age demographic. While this is not surprising, a skewing of age demographic in low-paying service-related industries is unsettling.

Most service sector businesses have a disproportionate number of women over 55. This often leads to mature women accepting jobs that involve weekend work; jobs rejected by younger employees who have families. Mature women are also more frequently employed in low end administration support jobs. They offer older men labor related manufacturing, construction, transportation, or public utility jobs.

For older job seekers who wish to start a new job, there are a few keys to success: involvement in sports and extra-curricular activities that send a message of youthfulness is a definite plus. Also, willing to go the extra mile definitely adds merit to your resume.

AARP (American Association of Retired Persons), an American non-profit organization serving people over fifty, lists fifty companies with pro-active hiring practices in recruiting, training, education, workplace adaptation, career development, flexible scheduling, pension and health benefits for the age of their workforce.

Some big box retailers are often more open to offering opportunities to mature workers. Often these jobs are physically exhausting, inappropriate for anyone with foot, knee, hip or back problems and hard work with a relatively low remuneration. Is this the answer, or a trade-off, for the mature worker who is looking for a low stress job with flexible hours?

Some employers are including benefits for part-time workers at the same level as for full-time workers. While this is a socially responsible move, it could mainly be a survival tactic reflecting a tight job market and employers experiencing difficulty finding and retaining employees. It may create the illusion of a good company to work for, without being a fulfilling and enjoyable place to work.

People at all life stages are recognizing the benefits of life balance. Employers who recognize employees as valuable to the success of the company, treat them with respect, and support their individual needs will inch ahead of their competition. They will attract employees who are more engaged in their work and, as a result, the company will benefit from better productivity.

Perception and reality end up on a collision course as soon as we relinquish our power and adopt the feeling of "I am a victim." There are opportunities where maturity is a plus. There are companies that appreciate maturity. The wise person recognizes that if they are seeking an employment opportunity, they need to identify the companies where they fit and release their frustration and anxiety over opportunities that don't fit.

It may be unrealistic to assume there is no Silver Ceiling; some age related biases are very evident. The challenge is to change those things we can, and not buy into victimhood based on the things we can't change. Our biggest barrier is that if we accept or see ourselves as 'older and less useful'—it becomes a self-fulfilling prophecy.

The Silver Ceiling is about to be shattered. Labour shortages are beginning to occur as increasing numbers of older employees retire, resulting in a need for employers to attract and retain older employees. Employers are suddenly crying out for mature responsible, knowledgeable, capable workers.

The demand for older workers, in certain sectors, will explode exponentially over the next ten years. Beyond employment, there are a myriad of opportunities for self-employment, contracting and entrepreneurial ventures. If the employment scene has lost its lustre, perhaps there are other opportunities that offer greater independence and are more suited to your present life stage.

Career or Income Earning Opportunities

Retirees need to utilize transferable skills from their life-careers to create new careers or extensions of their pre-retirement career. For some it can come from consulting within the same industry. For others the choice is a small entrepreneurial venture - others choose to take monstrous risks and launch major corporations. Risk is still risk, even if you have years of experience.

Joseph M. (Jody) Grant, a Texan with a Texan-styled idea for retirement, retired at 59 and founded a bank. He later wrote his book ***The Great Texas Banking Crash: An Insider's Account*** telling the story of a decision by the FDIC (Federal Deposit Insurance Corporation) and the devastating consequences to his bank. Business ventures can come with risks outside our personal control and while a business venture can be a rewarding way to spend the Segue Years, due caution needs to be emphasized.

In the US, SCORE (Service Corps of Retired Executives), provides assistance to individuals starting businesses. They will assist with operating, cash flow forecasts and budgeting. Similarly in Canada, federally funded Small Business Service Centres provide a wealth of information and help for people starting businesses. There are more work-at-home opportunities than ever before. Some opportunities have minimal returns on investment, at best.

Others can be lucrative. Sales ability and business management skills are helpful for anyone who wants to explore entrepreneurial ventures.

CHAPTER 6

LIFE ARENAS:

AREAS FOR CHOICES AND GROWTH

The strongest principle of growth lies in human choice.

George Eliot (1819 - 1880)

Compartmentalizing the areas of your life allow you to focus and achieve an easy transition to the lifestyle of your dreams. Areas that need attention are financial, health, relationships (with self, family or others), career or work reorientation, social, leisure, spirituality and sexuality. Let's explore these life arenas.

Financial Security

Some analysts state that 70% of your working income is unnecessary. This is welcome news to people who do not have the retirement savings they had hoped to accumulate. Some analysts suggest replacing part of your income through part-time ventures. With $370,000 in savings, a couple can retire at age 55. By the time you reach 60, the amount falls to $315,000. To retire at 62, you only need $260,000. These figures are calculated to provide an annuity income of $35,000 per annum prior to the age when government pensions kick in. When combined with pensions, the annuity can generate a livable income for most people who have no mortgage payments or dependents.

According to the EBRI (Employee Benefit Research Institute) Retirement Confidence Survey, 40% of workers have saved less than $50,000 (not including their primary residence and defined benefit plans). Based on people 55+ they report:

- 26% have less than $10,000 saved
- 14% have less than $50,000
- 22% have less than $149,000 9% have between $150,000 and $249,000
- 11% have between $250,000 and $499,000
- only 17% have more than $500,000

This report also states that only 41% of people aged 55+ are confident they will have enough money to survive their remaining years. Startling also is that 60% of Canadians, according to Statistics Canada, have no pension plan and depend on Canada Pension and Old Age Security.

With that computing to a maximum of $15,606 annually, most retirees are not basking in the sun at tropical resorts, nor traveling nearly as much as they assumed they would when they cleaned out their desk for the last time. It is a situation that could cause despair and we will discuss solutions when we discuss sustainable lifestyles for the Segue Years.

Health is Wealth

Aiming for good health is good advice at any age. Many diseases and illnesses can be prevented or at least delayed significantly by participating in physical activity, and having regular health check-ups with a chiropractor, naturopath or other preventative health care practitioner.

Disciplines and remedies many centuries old–such as Chinese medicine, are proving to have scientific validity. You ultimately have the choice of being proactive and involved in preventing illness and deterioration of your body or supporting the mega-buck pharmaceutical companies.

Michael Moore's movie ***Sicko*** was perhaps the first of many movies that questioned our healthcare systems and choices. Netflix features many health related documentaries. An increasing number of documentaries including ***Forks over Knives, A Users Guide to Cheating Death, The C Word, Game Changers*** and others portray various sides of the healthcare challenges and debates.

These movies, at the very least, provoke thought about our health care choices and systems. If the pharmaceutical companies have endless financial resources and spend millions of dollars on promoting their philosophies and products –does that make their point of view and research more valid than the preventative health practitioners who have limited budgets to promote their point-of-view? Does money talk? Who do you want to believe? What long-term impact are the beliefs you adopt going to have on your health and longevity?

A woman I once knew had a serious heart attack during her early fifties. She changed her diet and lifestyle. She used natural remedies. She also refused gall bladder surgery, choosing rather to use a natural treatment. For many years I thought of her as eccentric.

However, years have spoken for themselves. She lived to be over 100. I know several others who after serious health problems in their forties or fifties adopted alternative medicine approaches and lived into their late nineties.

You owe it to yourself to educate yourself. With the abundance of information available on the internet – the difficulty is differentiating between information of value and information created only to generate sales. We live in an information age; indifference and other forms of ignorance don't cut it. There is value in both the traditional medical approach and alternative healthcare, with prevention being the priority.

I am not medically trained nor trained in natural medicine. I am not in a position to guide your choices. However, I am convinced it is our responsibility to educate ourselves, research information and think critically.

Relationship with Self

When the self identity acquired from one's career ends, people who have relied on their work as the major defining factor in their identity face an identity crisis. They find they do not really know themselves, other than as defined through work. With that identity comes social connections and a sense of being a valuable contributor to society.

We often identify ourselves by the hats we wear. Women who have dedicated themselves to child rearing may similarly suffer from empty nest syndrome. The Segue Years involve a shift from a life focused on a career to a life without work and often call for a redefinition of self.

The degree to which we are in touch with ourselves determines the level of difficulty we may encounter in this aspect of transition. The more engaged a person is with their career and the longer they have worked in one career, the more likely they are to see themselves, largely or in part, as the title on their business card. Although this has historically been a problem for men, increasing numbers of women are now leaning toward a personal identity that reflects their workplace roles.

Besides the sense of identity, your relationship with self includes being forgiving, understanding and honoring your likes and dislikes, and being true to your convictions. During your working years, you may suppress your opinions or values in order to fulfill the role expected in the corporate setting.

It is possible to become numb to your own feelings. It is equally possible to become your own worst critic, constantly invalidating your efforts and as a result causing yourself undue stress. Do you really understand your personality type and do you provide opportunities to exercise your dominant traits? Understanding ourselves and our traits at any life stage helps us effectively design a lifestyle that will fit.

Charles came out of retirement to start a consultant business. He helps people solve their career challenges. Using a personality inventory tool, he helps his clients understand how temperament and traits can relate to how we manage interpersonal relationships or conflict management in the workplace. Understanding temperaments and traits can help identify good career choices.

Better self-understanding and self-expression can occur right where we are in life. When we understand the motives from which we and others act, we can become more effective and less stressed. The time required to refocus your energies away from survival into thriving, can alter your perception of your current situation.

Through working with a coach who uses various emotional intelligence or personality inventory profiles, it is possible to reengage in the workplace while better enjoying the remaining years at work. It is an illusion to think all interpersonal problems and emotional struggles will end the last day you walk out the door of your job. The workplace provides an opportunity to develop the coping skills we will need in our personal lives and later in life.

While Charles is an example of an entrepreneur whose later-in-life business is giving him an opportunity to work at something he loves, he does this by helping people become more successful in the workplace. For some, working is something they need to commit to for five, ten, or fifteen years after traditional retirement age.

If this is the right choice for you, do not to be influenced by the lure to disengage from the workplace prematurely. While many people shift to an entrepreneurial lifestyle after leaving traditional employment, entrepreneurship isn't for everyone.

Relationships and Social Connectedness

Human beings are social animals. Social isolation can be a major factor leading to depression. Social connectedness is important and allows us an opportunity to see ourselves through the eyes of others; even more so when we hear our own words when expressing our opinions.

Nathan, a successful businessman, was stating his opinion about a political event. He stopped halfway through and said, "Wow, I sound like my dad—that isn't really what I think." Expressing his point of view verbally resulted in his recognizing that his intellectual point of view and his emotional point of view were out of sync. This is an example of the benefit of social connections. Awareness is the first step in changing our beliefs and behaviors.

Research also seems to show that there is a difference between relationships with relatives and friends. In fact, we are healthiest when we maintain blood-relative connectedness, a minimum of three close friendships and numerous casual friends or acquaintances. Blood-relative connectedness doesn't mean you have to be bosom buddies with curmudgeonly Uncle Joe or neurotic Aunt Matilda. It means having a connection to at least one or two people who link you to your roots. Roots keep us grounded and bring a sense of security.

We all need a sense of community and connectedness. Relationships are important to well-being. In generations gone by, the nuclear family supported the needs of its members through the years from infancy to the elderly.

The concept of retirement homes, seniors' lodges, adult daycares and other methods of housing seniors is a concept that has evolved over the past forty years. The increase in the divorce rate has created blended families. Many families now have mothers, fathers, step-mothers, step-fathers, step-in-laws, half-brothers, half-sisters, brothers, sisters, step-sisters and step-brothers.

While families connect in the most complex web imaginable, there is less connectedness and more confusion about the roles of family. As society continues to redefine itself, retirees are facing the challenge of redefining their familial expectations during Segue Years.

When responsibilities extend to aging parents and dependent adult children, communication is the key. It is like sex education. Too often we put off "the talk" until an issue arises, making it even more difficult to discuss as they have already made certain decisions.

Understanding one another's expectations and beliefs is the key to any family communication issues. Family members can assume that other members of the family should be able to understand them, even if they don't explain their feelings.

Likewise, it can be easy for younger generations to believe their point-of-view is the right choice, with no dialogue with the senior. Personalities and life experience play a huge role in what works for one person and what doesn't. It is unfair to set oneself up as a decision maker regarding what is best for a parent, if we were not willing to the desires of the parent, while the parent could express their opinions.

It may be easy to see aging parents as incompetent and may conclude there is no validity to any of their wants or wishes with it comes to their living arrangements during their final years.

Allowing parents to have dignity includes considering their point-of-view. Sometimes it may require you to be open-minded and may call on you to grant wishes that may, to your way of thinking, seem unwise.

When it comes to communication, guesswork is the most inefficient way to manage a relationship. It isn't possible to guess what another person is thinking or feeling. Having family meetings to discuss what is going well and what changes they would like to see, can assist with addressing problems before they become issues that have escalated into an all out crisis. Like a car, relationships will break down if you do not do regular maintenance.

Retirement coaches can assist individuals and/or couples in defining their plan to have a happy and enjoyable retirement. The first step in communicating your expectations to your family - not only for the near future but also for your *l'età dell'oro* (golden or bonus years) is to identify and articulate your own life plan.

This includes candid recognition of your familial relationships and a willingness to openly express your needs and expectations and the expectations of family members. During these discussions, we base opinions on perspectives. Does the opinion of the caregiver respect the desires of the person in care? It can cause unwarranted depression for the senior if their opinions are not respected in decisions that affect them.

Relationships are built on trust and respect, and it is easier to maintain a relationship than it is to rebuild from the shambles after neglect. Criticism and confrontational approaches never win respect. If you value the relationship, be willing to do the work necessary to keep it healthy.

Career and Independence from Career

We have already discussed moving to greater independence from careers. While we assume it will be easy to adjust to not working, most people experience a honeymoon phase with their new-found freedom, only to find they miss working.

Work gives us a sense of identity, a sense that we are contributing to society—giving our activities a sense of meaning, social connection, and financial gain. These can contribute to psychological well-being.

Interacting with our peers and business associates forms a sounding board for our personal frustrations, our hopes and aspirations and to help us make sense of life's experiences. This social connection provided by the workplace is important. It needs replacing when we leave the workforce. We become accustomed to the time pressures exerted by work schedules and through balancing work and personal lives. This forces us into time management. Some people find that after leaving the workforce, they lack the motivation to maintain a schedule and soon find their days filled with meaningless activities.

Here again, the concept of retirement as being a segue rather than an event alleviates many of these challenges. If the transition from working full time is to part-time, an entrepreneurial venture or volunteering, it is easier to develop a new identity, continued time management, a social outlet and the sense that your time is for a worthy cause. Discussions about career decisions, part-time work and volunteering will help you explore options and provide an opportunity to determine what will fit best for you.

Leisure

Some people have an endless list of interests, hobbies and sports and life just never seems to give them time to participate at the level they wish to participate during their working years. For these people there is little danger of lacking leisure.

For others who will tell you they never had time for any hobbies or interests during their working years, the story is very different. It seems they lack the ability to connect with their creative side, have failed to develop an interest in physical activities, and are not that interested in the intellectual side of life. Some of them fit the title of DBA (dead before arrival) or LD (living dead). This is a simple lack of passion and zest. They have a much higher likelihood of becoming disillusioned with life after they leave the workforce. If this strikes a chord, it is time to work on your leisure life—prior to handing in your resignation letter.

Leisure is any activity we do when we have nothing to do. Kate laments that compared to others, she has no leisure activities. However, she reads at least one book a week; she gardens and she has a poodle. Leisure doesn't have to be pleasure cruises in the Caribbean, or heli-skiing in the Rocky Mountains. Leisure needs to fit your personality, and while there are health benefits from part of your leisure being from a physical activity, it should always be something fun for you—otherwise the enjoyment factor will not be there.

Unfortunately, some retirees change leisure activities into chores. When a pastime such as golf, gardening, home renovations, or other hobbies or activities taken too seriously, become work. Sometimes people will think using their hobby as a part-time income is a great idea, but time pressures, need for achievement and long hours can turn pleasure and leisure into work or even stress.

Golfers elevate their stress by attempting to lower their handicap. Gardeners set high expectations or engage in work that is heavy and difficult until they turn their dream garden into a nightmare that consumes their life and stresses them out.

Spirituality

Spirituality is that which connects us to something bigger than ourselves, providing a sense of security, and the ability to see the BIG picture. It is the sense of connection and acceptance of a higher power. Spirituality enables us to see beyond our mortal experience to possibilities beyond the limited thinking we engage in if we focus only on ourselves. It is the sense that the decisions we make impact others, our community, our world and the universe.

Spiritual groundedness enables us to accept our limitations, form philosophies relating to coincidences, accept the "laws of the universe" and develop a value system. It enables us to accept that bad things happen – even to good people. Even good people can't dive out of an airplane, at cruising altitude, and expect gravity to honor their needs. It is an inner sense of knowing – the feeling *in your gut*, or *in your heart* – the sense that everything will be okay. It is trust, faith and freedom from doubt.

Sexuality

Sexuality is not a life-stage! It is a natural part of the human experience—even among the elderly. Humans are sexual beings, and the desires of wanting to be touched and loved are much more alive among the elderly than you may believe. Older adults can continue to enjoy a healthy, happy sex life especially if love, respect, and communication are present; and even better if they are soul mates, best friends, and both partners have healthy attitudes toward sexuality.

The sexual response cycle–comprising arousal, plateau, orgasm and resolution—relies on mental attitudes and physical responses. Physical health problems involving sexual response organs or other health issues may impair certain sexual activities.

However, it is likely that mental attitudes play a larger role in sexual arousal and satisfaction among consenting adults than physical factors do. A healthy mind-set toward sexual expression probably plays more of a major role in sexual enjoyment than physical aspects do at any age.

We often attribute impaired sexual performance to physical problems, and mental attitude or sexuality issues are too often overlooked. The greatest ally of mid-life and older adults is education to understand physiological changes in the body. From puberty to old age, we live in changing bodies; Understanding and knowledge are keys to healthy attitudes.

Men over 50 often experience slower physical expression and erectile response to stimulation. Should either partner become anxious or panic when response requires a few minutes versus several seconds, it may end any possibilities.

We are all spammed with emails from modern drug pushers who prey on performance anxiety—turning it into a billion dollar industry. Their constant hype may escalate self-doubt into anxiety quickly leading to a self-fulfilling prophecy in the sex-life of the reader.

According to the Wall Street Journal (Tara Parker-Hope) "More than 20 million men around the world use it regularly. In the US, one out of every five men over 40 has tried it. An average of nine Viagra pills are dispensed every second."

Not everyone who takes it benefits—50% of men do not refill their prescriptions. In fact 66% of men given Viagra compared to 25% of men given placebos experienced favorable results. Men with erectile dysfunction because of psychological issues fared best.

Many who found benefits had other health issues, including vascular disease (88%) and those suffering from depression (86%). The remaining categories include men with hypertension (75%), diabetes (70%), ischemic heart disease (69%) and those who've had their prostate removed (47%) according to Pfizer studies and the Wall Street Journal.

The skeptic is quick to question the accuracy of any study completed by an organization with a vested interest in the results. A study in the British Journal of Ophthalmology stated men were 10 times as likely as the comparison group, to suffer from optic nerve damage (diagnosed as non-arteritic anterior ischaemic optic neuropathy—NAION) if they had taken Cialis or Viagra.

Sometimes it isn't until years later, that some drugs are pulled because of serious side-effects. Pharmaceutical companies are focused on profit. When do profits come before long-term patient well-being? All too often people are taking more drugs to deal with the side effects of the drugs they are prescribed.

Our culture often trivializes the sexual pleasure attained from touching to talking and being physically close—glamorizing intercourse with orgasm to be all that matters. Individuals differ, as do their desires, and other factors including partner availability and preference contribute to determining sexual release choices.

Older women continue to enjoy sexual pleasure. Women commonly desire longer foreplay and hormonal changes can cause slower arousal or decreased lubrication, increasing the need and a desire for longer foreplay. The post menopausal woman, no longer faced with the possibility of an unwanted pregnancy, can experience a sense of greater freedom.

Women can enjoy arousal and orgasm even into their golden years. When a woman understands and verbalizes her needs, and she has a responsive partner who is interested in fulfilling her needs—sexual pleasure can continue to be mutually enjoyed. Masters and Johnson advocated continued sexual activity among older adults. They stated, "There is a tremendous physiological and psychological value in continuity of sexual exposure."

Perhaps one of the risk factors that threatens sexual intimacy in a long-term relationship or marriage is complacency and the assumption that one partner *should know* (be able to guess) what the other partner wants or needs. That doesn't work in any other aspect of a relationship. Why would it work in sexual encounters?

Perhaps the biggest challenge, from a sexuality point-of-view, for un-partnered Boomers and seniors seeking a new relationship is finding someone with compatible sexual desires and attitudes. Combine this need with the challenge of finding a compatible personality, who is intellectually and spiritually attuned and it is no wonder it is difficult to find the right partner later in life.

The reality is, sexuality is a normal part of life and the more comfortable we are in discussing it with our loved one, and trusted professionals, the more likely we are to be fulfill and enjoy our sexual desires. There are only two kinds of people—those who are enjoying their sexuality and those who wish they had more sexual intimacy in their lives.

Choices Relating to Life Arenas

Based on the arenas we have discussed, it is easy to see how our choices in one area of our life can affect other areas of our life. We make some of our choices based on life circumstances, responding to our needs or sometimes more reactive. Sometimes it's easier to see our options and other times we feel less able to make choices because of the perception that certain things are out of our control. It is more likely that they are lower on our priority list.

Nevertheless, our status or the circumstances we have created by past decisions alter the choices we have available to us at a given time. Occasionally, existing circumstances will change as we make decisions in other life arenas. Choices, for example, about where we live often depend on our marital status. The choices we make relating to health are influenced by present health challenges. The key is to recognize the areas where we can most successfully enact meaningful change and often the benefits spill over into all life areas.

CHAPTER 7

MAKING THE SHIFT:

DESTABILIZATION TO REVITALIZATION

Human beings, by changing the inner attitudes of their minds, can change the outer aspects of their lives.

William James (1842 - 1910)

The first time they call us upon to discover ourselves is as teenagers. This is often a difficult time: raging hormones, sorting out the various philosophies of our peers and the plethora of options that confront us in the career world. At the same time we are separating from parents and testing our own wings. The same questioning faces us as we come to our Segue Years – often driven by an increased awareness of our mortality.

The number of people retiring in the next 15 years is unprecedented. In the next twenty years more than 25% of the present population of Canada will leave their jobs and enter retirement. Approximately 83 million Americans are Baby Boomers. The US Census predicts that by 2012 there will be 21 million job vacancies with only 17 million bodies available to fill them.

This for many is more frightening than graduation day. There is a huge stigma to retirement and men especially have a difficult time with this transition, as they have often obtained a lot of their life meaning from their work.

The Segue Years are a new beginning. Those who are unprepared experience a loss of self-worth, an end of their contribution; a sense of emptiness seems to quickly follow on the heels of the planned vacation, or Retirement Honeymoon. "What NOW?" they wonder. The importance of engaging in formal planning for this transition is not merely a good idea; it can make a significant difference in the lives of both the retiree and their family.

Harvey managed 25 employees for 20 years and came home to retirement; he quickly started to apply his management skills to his marriage and home. The trouble was Elisa, his wife, had been a stay-at-home wife and mother for 30 years and could quite manage their home. Instead of treating his marriage and home as the latest corporate merger, Harvey eventually learned to channel his skills and interests into a meaningful volunteer position.

He experienced an increased sense of purpose and it enabled Elisa and Harvey to redefine their relationship in a way that suited both of them and their new found lifestyle.

Garth and Deidre, a childless couple married 35 years, did not communicate or come to compromise as they faced their transition to retirement and it ended woefully. Deidre was a successful career nurse and her employer enforced mandatory retirement at age 65. She loved her hobby farm and animals of all types and she looked forward to spending her retirement volunteering with disabled children and animals.

Garth's plans were far different. He wanted to sell their property and sail around the world. Deidre hated sailing and particularly on stormy seas. Deidre became so disillusioned with the prospects of what her future held that she lapsed into a serious depression and one day she took her own life.

Deidre saw no solutions. Less than a year later, mandatory retirement ended.

One symptom of depression is a feeling of hopelessness. Unfortunately, Deidre needed help. She needed someone to listen to her, and she needed the help of resources. She faced what seemed like an insurmountable obstacle. Whether she needed a fresh beginning on her own or help to bridge the gap between Garth and her perspective, she didn't get the help she needed. Reaching out is difficult, but so necessary if you are struggling emotionally.

Each of us has an individual set of challenges, skills, strengths, and weaknesses. This could be the caregiving for aging dependent parents and/or adult children who are dependent or attending school. Others may have health issues, a lack of hobbies, or feeling that life has little meaning without a job.

Dr. Richard Johnson, psychologist and retirement expert, differentiates between career and job. He defines career as a person's passion and purpose in life, while a job is what a person does day-after-day. It is an interesting differentiation. From that point of view many people spend their working years working at a J.O.B. - Just Over Broke—to defray expenses in hopes of 'having a life' after age 65 only to find out they are still just over broke, and all that has changed is that the alarm clock never rings.

This provides a strong argument in favor of taking action to create a career plan long before retirement. It is never too late to start living a planned life. Using a Life Plan - similar to a Business Plan - increases the likelihood of achieving one's dreams and achieving them with less effort. The difference between those who '*exist*' or drift though life without direction and those who live their dreams is knowing what they want, writing a plan, and staying on course—retirement coaches assist people to achieve these tasks.

The sooner, and more consistently we work on getting to know ourselves and the sooner we become who we authentically are, the sooner we live the life of our dreams. Self-discovery is an ongoing process and the greatest celebration of life available.

Some people lack adaptability and hang on to things that make them feel secure. This is problematic when one is nearing the end of a career. Stalling can cause forced decisions and usually decisions that are forced upon us are more difficult to adapt to. It can change a natural segue into a crisis or devastating experience. Some people sadly lose the focus of their destination, then rationalize that the destination wasn't that important, and just give up. They suppress their truth. Some people who do this become overwhelmed with fear and disappointment. Eventually, it results in apathy, or they erupt in uncontrolled insecurities, cynicism, and bitterness.

For some individuals, emotional pain is turned inward, causing depression. For others, the pain is exhibited outwardly, in the form of aggression. Generally speaking, depression and passivity are more common in women; while anger and aggression are more often exhibited by men. Either way, this is avoiding reality. When we do not want to deal with the present, we first build fences, then walls. The building blocks for these walls are false beliefs and rationalizations.

The more conservative your personality type the more likely you are to resist change. Some people are natural risk takers and thrive on change. Others find it overwhelming and lack the skills to deal with inevitable segues in life. We can be immobilized either by failure to recognize our own self-destructive behaviors as inappropriate, immobilized by fear, or by lack of direction.

CHAPTER 8

READY OR NOT:

CONTEMPLATION TO DECISION

The self is not something ready-made,
but something in continuous
formation through
choice of action.
John Dewey (1859 - 1952)

To really enjoy life we must develop the skill Tarzan and the monkeys in the jungle use. Once they have a grasp of where they are going they swing free and disengage from the security of the past. They move with agility and purpose. Taking out the guesswork and having a clear focus of the next step is all it takes to swing through the jungle. It isn't necessary to have all the answers—just enough information to make the next leap of faith.

Approaching the Segue Years assuming the good life will just spontaneously begin the day we exit the office for the last time may result in just drifting for a while—with no real destination and at first this may seem okay. After all we have earned a good holiday; it is likely we will enjoy a Retirement Honeymoon. It will be great for a while. No alarm clock to wake us from our slumber - no responsibility. How can that not be a great way to live?

HR administrators frequently state that most retirees leave work excited about a motor home trip they are taking across the country, or their intentions to move to a retirement home, or to do renovations and catch up on the jobs in their job jar. During the first year or two after retirement they seem quite happy, and often stay in touch--then they drift out of the picture. When co-workers or HR administrators meet up with these retirees five years down the line, there are many who have become increasingly discontent with retirement.

What is going to happen when the honeymoon is over? Work has filled almost one third of our waking hours for 30 or more years of our life. With that we have come to identify ourselves by our job. It gives us some sense of meaning and it becomes to a great extent 'who we are.' Now we are in the process of redefining ourselves. Retirees are disappointed if they settle for defining their lives by default.

Equally ineffective is the decision to accept *good enough*. "I'm okay! So what if I am one degree off course; it isn't possible to predict the future anyway." A life without a destiny is like a ship without modern navigational tools. We now have GPS and to set sail out into open seas without GPS is unthinkable. Why would we not choose the best navigational system available? Assume a sailor sets sail westward, into the setting sun, and strays one degree further off course every day. In ninety days the boat would be sailing for the polar ice cap. If the boat survives the icebergs and continues on this course for a year, straying only one degree per day, the sailor would be right back to where he started.

Ironically, Columbus made a great discovery even though he had incomplete information. He started out not knowing where he was going. When he arrived, he had no idea where he was! When he got back, he didn't know where he had been - and he did it with someone else's money! Well, it worked for Columbus, but it isn't likely to work for us - unless we plan to explore somewhere other than planet earth!

The steps in developing meaningful transitions and change can be broken down into the following stages:

- Acceptance of Responsibility
- Perspective Testing
- Accepting Loss
- Contemplation
- The Decision
- Action Plan
- Re-evaluation

Acceptance of Responsibility

Many people have a good idea of what they want, and want to develop a plan that will convert their dreams into reality. Others lack adaptability and the ability to be self-directed. These people must get *unstuck.*

The transition from career to the lifestyle you choose to live during your Segue Years is a process, not an event. The more you choose to be involved in managing the dynamics of the process, the less often you will face the consequences of involuntary change. Yes, involuntary change occurs – for everyone. There will be unforeseeable events; some will be pleasant surprises, others not so – unforeseen events may include illness or tragedy. Many events assumed to be unforeseeable can be predicted. For instance, if we pay no attention to our health and then develop a degenerative disease, can we consider that to be an unforeseeable event?

Does that mean the expectation is perfection? We all fall short of applying everything we know, about health, for instance. It only means that we want to be informed decision makers. The action it requires may be obvious. *How to do it* may be within our ability. The resources we need may be at our fingertips. Sometimes, the task may seem unpleasant and rather than confront the situation, we attempt to hide from it or deny it.

Phil was starting a business as an architect and hired me as his coach. I could not understand why he didn't seem to make any progress. Then one day he said, "I need to show you something." He drew an office layout with 8 offices in the middle surrounded by a hall with offices along the opposite side of the hall. He drew the coffee station in the corner of the office.

He said, "Visualize a man starting at the coffeepot, and going to each office saying good morning to each person, going around the inside of the circle reaching the coffee pot by 10:00 AM and then refilling his coffee cup and visiting the offices on the opposite side of the hall, arriving back at the coffeepot by noon. After lunch he comes back and repeats the same routine."

"When will this man find the time to get his work done?" I asked.

"He doesn't. He just picks up the stuff from in his in-basket on his way past his office and then disburses it to other people as he passes by their offices."

"I don't think it would last long unless it was his duty to delegate the work to others. What about his performance review?"

"You can't point a finger at someone who makes no mistakes. If the person never puts their handwriting on any papers, there is no sign of work done shoddily or not done. The solution is never put your signature on anything. If you are going to do nothing—you need to *do nothing well*."

"You can't be serious. I don't see how the person could have any sense of satisfaction. I don't see how anyone could even want to do that. I don't understand the point you are trying to make?"

His response explained a lot. "Well, that is what I did for 20 years. I even got promoted to a manager without doing a thing. I was managing the department. It was a union environment and most of my promotions I achieved strictly based on seniority—and by making no enemies. In my entire life, I have never done any work."

He had spent 20 years collecting a paycheck from a government housing department—for doing nothing. Is it any wonder he had no sense of meaning in his life, and he had no work ethic or ability to help him launch his business as an architect? Worse yet, he had no desire to alter his behavior. He just wanted his wife to think he was trying hard to start his business. His wife was a teacher, and he wanted to keep her happy—in a few years they could both retire.

"Given this information, I don't feel coaching is of any benefit to you. I suggest we stop meeting," I responded. This was not what he intended to happen because of telling his story. He wanted me to support his inaction and to play his game to keep his wife happy.

What do <u>you</u> want? Mediocrity or excellence? The coach's motive is not to choose your path or to push you to take specific actions. Unwillingness to accept responsibility for one's actions results in stagnation. These people are only well-served by the coaching process if they have reached the point where they want to change the way they have been approaching life.

Perspective Testing

Perspective testing is the next part of the change process. We base most of our decisions on our perception. We need to have the flexibility and willingness to shift our perception when we learn new information that shows us our perception is not accurate or helpful to our progress. Our perception is our reality.

Sometimes it supports growth and fulfilment, sometimes it doesn't. Perception is powerful and exists everywhere in the decision making processes. Even when we use facts and we are analytical by nature or by process, we still use our perception to interpret the facts. Our perceptions either feed our anxieties or provide us with information for positive action.

The following story demonstrates how perceptions can feed anxieties and how different perceptions can form in the same situation. Three adults had been out waterskiing. Jared, the boat owner, discovered that the taillights on the boat trailer were not working, and after 20 minutes of tinkering, he could only think of getting home as fast as possible—before dark.

It was already too late—at best he would have darkness for the last 20 minutes, but he rationalized that by that time he would be on well-lit freeways as they neared the city. From his perspective, he feared a ticket or worse yet someone clipping his prize new boat.

From Tracy's viewpoint, finding a restaurant was the top priority—eventually she settled for phoning ahead to have pizza delivered upon their arrival home.

As it grew dark, Melissa, the third adult, grew increasingly anxious. From her perspective, she feared someone could clip the boat and cause the SUV and boat to jack-knife. It intensifies as Jared's decision to get himself between two 18 wheelers. His anxieties escalated as he jostled for position between semis, to evade the eyes of the four state troopers along the route. While this is a story of what-not-to-do, it ended okay with piping hot pizza delivered to the door upon their safe arrival.

Who perceived the situation most accurately? How effective were the perceptions in providing meaningful solutions? The point is, how often do we find ourselves in situations where we must decide and even though we have a strong point-of-view, we fail to honor our own values—choosing to say nothing?

How many times do we have a less than healthy perspective and instead of solving the problem we barge forward in the face of trouble? Do we try to change the perspective of others to match our less than healthy perception? Do others pressure us to accept their less than healthy perspective, and if we adopt it, why?

Perspectives influence all our decisions, including our work. People who live by default, assuming they are victims of circumstances, repeat the same unproductive behaviors again and again. Living by default or in survival mode is not good enough—we have the option of being so much more. Survival is what a victim does during a crisis. Decide to thrive. The attitude necessary for a thriving life is future-focused—the fuel of passion is the vision of something bigger and better than anything from the past.

According to psychologists, at least 80% of us come from dysfunctional backgrounds. Of 1000 successful people it is extremely likely many of them grew up in homes of alcoholics; where divorce or family disruptions rocked the home; or someone diagnosed them with learning disabilities. Sometimes overcoming difficulties can fuel an unstoppable desire to make more out of life. AND, if people who were 'statistically' unlikely to be successful, succeed—why can't we? We too - can do it.

Our perception determines our beliefs. Belief plus emotion equals results. Those things we believe strongly enough to put our energy behind - we create. Recognize your beliefs, own them, and be willing to change them when presented with information that challenges the accuracy of your perceptions. Our perspective can cheat us out of enjoying the present and the future. Attachment to the past can stop us from seeing possibilities for the future. Emotions centred on fancifully romanticizing the past can also hold us back from creating the future of our dreams.

Emotions are catalysts for change. Although emotions have a purpose, perceptions based on raw emotion rather than facts, are usually flawed. Emotions, attached to our beliefs, move us toward action and create our reality. All action comes about through motivation and all motivation stems from emotion.

If you don't believe this, think about being caught in heavy traffic when you are already running late for an appointment. Most people in this situation obsess about being late. When someone cuts them off—it confirms their opinion that the traffic is disgusting. The typical response is to add anger to the mix. Now the belief that other drivers are idiots builds the emotion. Before long, the cycle leads to a domino effect. Deciding to take that *short-cut* that will save time—turns out to be the *long-cut*, and the more emotions get involved to support the beliefs, soon the situation escalates to create a critical mass—now it takes on a life of its own and creates exactly the reality we expect.

Recently, I was in this exact situation. I was running late. I took a short-cut and immediately found myself in even a worse situation. The traffic came to a complete stop. Using my cell phone, I called ahead to say I would be late by about 20 -25 minutes—a realistic estimation given my current location and the lack of movement in the traffic.

After hanging up I thought, now the pressure is off. I will just relax and let this take as long as it takes. Miraculously the stress dissolved, traffic improved, and I arrived only 3 minutes late based on the originally scheduled time.

Understanding our emotions and taking action that will enable us to maintain an emotionally safe environment is necessary for our well-being. Maintaining a negative emotional state is to deny ourselves emotional safety and well-being. Ignoring our emotions can be like installing a smoke detector in our home and then taking the battery out so we won't have to listen to it squeal when we burn our dinner. If we go to sleep at night without reconnecting the smoke detector, we are lulling ourselves into a false sense of security.

Shifting emotions using objectivity can enable us to make well-reasoned decisions. Separating yourself from environments that constantly destroy your state of well-being can be a necessary step in making progress. If our emotions are constantly aroused—in a negative way–we can either numb out or get out.

Get out is the door to the attitudinal shift toward a positive mindset that will lead to an improved situation. Emotional safety and positive emotions are the precursors for growth. It is very important to surround yourself with supportive people. This becomes even more important when you are facing challenging transitions.

Our perception has a lot to do with our willingness to take risk, to be adaptable, to see opportunities and to create life that will bring us satisfaction. We can choose to emphasize the positive aspects of even the most negative experiences. Obviously it would be beneficial to enhance memories of positive aspects and minimize negative aspects of the experience.

Flexibility and adaptability are crucial factors in a successful retirement. This transition requires even more flexibility than we have needed at any other stage of life. It comes with more variables that we could perceive as negative and overwhelming. We may fear losing our independence or ability to function physically like we did when we were younger. We can either accept the aging process or we can resist it. Resisting it will not make it easier. It will not prevent it. The only influence we can exert on the aging process is to engage in physical and mental activities that keep us younger longer. We can also engage in a youthful mental attitude.

Initially taking a different perspective may seem difficult, then it will reach a point where the momentum builds, and results will be experienced. The positive change has a synergistic effect. If we wait until we are forced to act, it often comes at the cost of the action being more difficult. Both obligation and intention can be fuel sources for achieving goals. However, obligation is to coal, as intention is to hydrogen-powered fuel cells.

The motivators we choose in life can create smoke and be inefficient or be powerful and efficient. The choice is ours. When we are fuelled by pure high efficiency energy sources, things we scarcely even dare to dream about can become a reality with little effort.

Accepting Loss

All change requires you to accept loss. Even positive change results in loss. Sometimes the unwillingness to accept the need to let go of the security of the workplace can cause resistance. A career is like an old pair of runners—a long history, a journey of many miles, satisfactory performance, and comfortable. We want to keep them in case the new ones give us blisters and continue to keep them because they might come in handy if it is muddy.

Letting go may not be easy. If we feel deprived in life, we may want to keep things. We rationalize. Maybe someday we will be thankful to wear those tattered old things—even though we know that will not happen to us again. The same applies to fear. We know fear serves no beneficial purpose. We hang on to the fear, anyway.

Change causes, at least momentarily, insecurity as we let go of the old to allow room for the new. When we see value in the change or in what we are creating, it is easier to deal with the sense of loss. However, not all change holds the same appeal. It is natural to resist changes we don't want. Loss of loved ones, or our independence, is part of life. Many things in life are not easy.

It is more difficult to deal with those kinds of losses than the kind that can seem like a trade-off for a more ideal life experience. Both voluntary and involuntary change creates loss and learning effective strategies for dealing with loss is a necessary life skill. There are times to mourn, and there are times to move on. Knowing how to be your own best friend and learning the grace to allow yourself to heal promotes well-being and develops resilience.

Contemplation

Contemplation is *thinking it over before you act.* Contemplation is a perfectly normal stage in the change process. People often have difficulty with this stage, which can be one of the most productive times to work with a coach. It may seem that you are stuck, but you just need to process the next step before making the move to take action.

Thinking it over takes time. This is one of the biggest transitions of our lives. It is at least as significant as graduation day. It is the open door to the future. While we can look through that door and see opportunity, we can only get a snapshot of the view that will unfold as we take steps out into this new terrain. There will be mountains and valleys. That is okay. We have faced mountains before. We expect them. We have faced valleys before. We expect them.

We have resilience built up from years of experience. We know that time changes things and even the most difficult experiences need not derail us permanently. We are master travellers, and the skills we have developed in one area of life give us the strength to endure the climb to the mountain top and to find some beauty in the valley even though the view may not be as far reaching as the view from a mountain top.

We know from life that sometimes the experience at hand can be overwhelming and that it may take years before we can look back and appreciate the lessons learned in the valley experiences. Even if you are presently feeling overwhelmed, take courage. The biggest break-through comes after feeling disoriented. Disorientation forces us to search deep for answers. Sometimes this reveals things we would never come to understand if we spent our life on the mountain top.

Contemplation is important. Don't rush it. You have an open door and while you want to explore the opportunities, it is okay to have apprehensions. It is okay to take your time to ensure that you make decisions you will not regret later. We know that the biggest accomplishments in our adult life took time to unfold. Contemplation is different from day dreaming. Day dreaming is idly engaging in thoughts we have no intention to act upon. Ensure that time you spend in contemplation is constructive.

Contemplation includes exploring, researching, trying things out, testing, self-reflection, evaluating one's values and other constructive thought processes that help make a decision. It is the stage where we know we want to do something and as we decide what that is, we move closer and closer to taking action.

One pitfall that lurks in the contemplative state is procrastination. We need to be honest with ourselves and recognize the difference between not having enough information and procrastination. Procrastination can spring from fear, or from an unwillingness to take responsibility. It has often been said that we sometimes fear success as much as we fear failure. Procrastination can also be caused by lack of vision or passion.

"Someday, I will decide on something to do during my retirement." "I don't have time now, but I want to take a holiday." "I will start an exercise plan next Monday"...on and on goes the list of good intentions. Procrastination becomes like a parasite, sucking the sustenance out of one's life purpose, leaving it empty and meaningless.

Procrastination results in a loss of integrity. Commitments become empty promises, and people who live like this often look for additional unhealthy ways to escape from the miserable reality they create for themselves. It may lead to addictions to work, alcohol or the "I can't wait until…." syndrome.

"I can't wait until the weekend." "I can't wait until I get a new sports car." "I can't wait until I get a new job." These or similar statements are examples of living in an illusion. Focussing on a fantasy causes the present to become a vacuum in their lives. There is no pleasure *in the moment* because it becomes a *necessary evil* - something that has to be endured until the magic moment of expectation arrives. This is really a dismal existence.

Procrastination occurs only because the vision of results is lacking, or because it seems like the effort exceeds the reward. It is the result of the faulty belief that *later is soon enough.* Before establishing an Action Plan, it is necessary to re-evaluate your beliefs and values. You must become aware of what you really believe.

You must remove the barriers caused by faulty beliefs and values before you can achieve your goals. Often on the surface we may think we believe certain things but upon a careful examination of our behaviors we can recognize a gap between our beliefs and actions. If there is a gap, it usually means we don't really believe what we say we believe—because if we did, our actions would support our beliefs.

Naturally, you want to prevent yourself from repeating painful experiences of the past. Attempts to set goals can lead to the discovery that goal setting is not the complete answer. The power of determination is never stronger than the power of belief. You cannot achieve goals incongruent with your internally held beliefs, values, and intentions.

Today is reality. Tomorrow's reality is determined by the actions, beliefs and/or values we live by today. Your vision becomes a reality with less effort once your beliefs and values congruently support your intentions and aspirations. Life no longer seems like a constant struggle. You are engaged in the flow of creation and it achieves accomplishments with ease.

When I think of the value we attach to things, I am reminded of a photo shoot of diamonds for a poster I was making. By networking, I found a young mother who had many expensive diamonds. I informed her that the photographer was also a police officer who did photography as a hobby on his days off.

She was willing to meet two total strangers in a park with $50K worth of diamonds. While she was not in danger, because the photographer was truly a police officer and our intentions were honest. It appalled him that she never questioned her safety. A motivated criminal could tell her the same story, and she would believe it. She did not ensure her own safety. When she arrived, she had several rings loose in the pocket of her bib-overall jean outfit.

During our time together, her five-year-old son summoned her to a brook to see tadpoles. The mother leaned over the water to view the tadpoles and one ring fell into the water. We were more concerned about its retrieval than she was.

Then she said, "These diamonds mean nothing to me. My husband always buys me a new diamond after I find out he has been having another affair. Really, I hate them because they are symbols of adultery." What do you value and why? It may also be good to ask, "What do you *not value*, but hang on to anyway?"

The Decision

The next step in the change process is the decision—the moment of clarity or epiphany. Decisions aren't easy. Any life-changing decision involves facing unknowns and has consequences. For many people, this can be a very clearly defining moment. They can even tell you years later where they were when they made the decision.

All the waffling, procrastination, and contemplation become a thing of the past. They KNOW where they are going. They see the goal and they are eager to start the process of getting there.

The bigger the transition, or the more stuck the person is, the more clearly they will know when they have arrived at a decision. They move from "I think I want…" to "I know I want." Their language is no longer filled with tentative words or uncertainty.

If you do not experience the decision as a clearly defined moment, it doesn't mean that you haven't arrived at a decision yet. Your decision may be less emotionally impacting if you are more objective and methodical in your personal decision making style or if you have been very close all along, and the moment is more about a decision to take action than it is a change of direction.

How self-reflective can influence how you experience your decision. Some people are less aware of their intuition, emotions, and felt senses. People who are tuned into their intuition feel it in their gut or heart. Paying attention to the physical responses in our bodies that relate to our emotions, thoughts and actions is a very revealing exercise. It certainly makes it clearer how many physical ailments evolve from emotion.

The Segue Years require strong decision-making skills. Statistics show individuals who work in structured work environments, with bureaucratic decision-making processes, have more difficulty with the transition to retirement than people who have followed an entrepreneurial career path. Entrepreneurs have been working in an environment where the awareness of the impact of their decisions permeates every aspect of their success. This better equips them to adapt to the constantly changing and self-managed lifestyle that freedom from work presents.

Making a decision doesn't mean that you see all the answers. People who make life-changing decisions have a vision. They know it will take a lot of work to get there. There may be fear, anticipation, anxiety, doubt, and questions; however, the biggest part of their future success has kicked in.

Passionate people are hard to stop. They achieve what they set out to do, despite naysayers and obstacles. Passionate people believe in what they are doing and feel it is a worthy cause. It matters very little to them how long it takes to achieve or what others think of their decision. They don't need as much validation from others. Their self-esteem rises.

Les said to his business partner, "I envy your passion. I have always wished I could experience passion. I have never had it. I see others who are passionate and I know it must feel a lot different to be doing something with passion, but I don't know how to become passionate. I just don't think it is part of my personality."

Passion is not dependent on personality type. It comes from commitment. Les was the most uncommitted person you could ask to meet. He avoided commitment in every aspect of his life.

Although Les was married for about 25 years, he had been an absentee husband for 23 years, repeatedly choosing to work hundreds of miles from home. In business, he was a follower and if he didn't agree with something, his approach was avoidance. If the workload increased - Les found a reason to become an absentee business owner by creating a perceived crisis somewhere more convenient—such as working for a friend who owned an eco-tourism company. Les had a history of short-lived business partnerships—it was not he who made the decision to part ways. He didn't make decisions. As a result he frequently had to react to changes as they occurred.

Like Phil the architect, Les was sociable, and both of them used their social charm to attract opportunities to get through life with little or no effort. On the surface these two men seemed happy. However, they were miserably unhappy. They denied themselves the fulfilment that striving and achieving brings.

Decisions bring commitment and commitment fuels passion. One of my mentors, Dr. Richard Barwell, says "Commit and the passion will follow." Passion comes from the Latin root word *passio*, which means *to suffer for*. People who have made a definite decision soon develop the passion. They commit to their decisions and that commitment enables them to make it happen.

Achieving satisfaction from life and solving your personal problems is an individual responsibility. Taking control and living the life of your dreams has huge rewards, no matter how difficult it is to imagine a life much different from the one you live today. Tarzan and his monkey friends understood. You must let go of the branch you are clinging to if you will swing through the jungle of life with ease.

CHAPTER 9

TAKING ACTION:

CONCEPT TO REALITY

He had discovered a great law of human action, without knowing it – namely, that in order to make a man or a boy covet a thing, it is only necessary to make the thing difficult to obtain.

Mark Twain (1835 – 1910),
"The Adventures of Tom Sawyer"

Clarity about what you intend to do with your life, and a strong sense of purpose will propel you forward more than any *Action Plan* or set of goals. If you know what you intend to do and have a clearly written *Statement of Intent*, it is easy to pull yourself back on track and into action. The Statement of Intent is the WHY, and each action you take can be placed against that mirror to determine if it will move you toward the WHY.

As you take action, your actions become the HOW. Successful people have an Action Plan. They chart their path and have a dynamic living plan that they revisit frequently to stay on target and to ensure they do not lose focus. Besides helping with focus, it leads to better time management and decision making. It prevents you from making decisions based on negative emotions that could spring from the heat of the moment. An Action Plan helps keep your dream alive. It provides milestones and a way of organizing yourself.

Action Plans must be dynamic, cover contingencies, and include strategies for success. Goals, while they can support your action, have less power than the purpose and passion behind your actions. Goals are only effective when they can monitor your progress.

Sometimes we chase goals that are unachievable because the goal posts are not stationary. Not only is this disappointing, it is very frustrating. Measuring progress against moving, or inappropriate goal posts, results in failure. While progress is never a straight-forward process, and small deviations are normal, we want to avoid lack of progress or going off on a tangent.

We need to recognize the difference between flexibility and instability. Flexibility is the ability to adapt to a variety of circumstances. Instability is the inability to remain committed when distractions provide new alternatives or challenges. Frequent deviations, or an extreme inability to stay focused may be indicators of physical or mental health issues and consulting a doctor or counsellor can be advisable. as well as it might, and move it to the next level.

Acceptance is the Key

Acceptance is a crucial factor in moving beyond the barriers that hold us back in life. Acceptance applies on many different levels and can provide a foundation that helps us sort out the difference between real and perceived barriers and can help us establish realistic goals. As we look at acceptance we will explore it from the inside out, beginning on a personal level and moving toward acceptance of external factors

Acceptance of Self

Often we become our own worst critic. By assimilating the opinions and expectations of others, we establish a set of beliefs about what we should be. *Should* is like a pair of shackles that inhibit our ability to act. It is founded in a belief that we have obligations, and that we are falling short of meeting those obligations.

This implies failure, before we have even begun. Think through what you really expect of yourself and the gap between what you think you *should be,* and what you *are* becomes much less apparent.

By removing the expectations of others, we are able to savor the things we appreciate most and self-acceptance becomes easy. Suddenly, we realize we have something to offer, we value our own accomplishments and we are less self-critical. Self acceptance is vital to inner peace, relieves stress, and is conducive to personal growth. Self acceptance enables us to deal with the external factors that impact our decisions. It makes it okay to be you. Accept where you are at any given time, allow yourself to make the most of your strengths and to forgive your imperfections.

Acceptance of Responsibility

Although we have already discussed responsibility, a few comments as to responsibility from the point of view of acceptance are relevant. Some belief systems allow a lot of room for denial of personal contribution to one's own successes and struggles.

Many belief systems are based on fate, predestination or on the theory that humans are, at best, prone to failure and defeat. These beliefs provide excuses for those who are unwilling to take responsibility for their own behavior.

Take advantage of opportunities that lead to personal growth. There are hard ways and easy ways to learn lessons. Any time we can learn from the experience of others without having to go through a hardship is a short-cut to personal growth. Maturity is not based on age - it is the end result of learning from life.

Acceptance of a Situation

One only needs to look at a person such as Rick Hansen, who wheeled his wheelchair a distance equivalent to the circumference of the earth to raise awareness and generate funds for spinal cord research, to know it isn't the circumstance one finds oneself in, it is what you do with those circumstances. Rick was an athletic 15-year-old when he was injured in a motor vehicle accident.

It always makes me feel very humble when I see the courage and enthusiasm people like this engage in to further a cause against all odds. They have the courage to do something most able-bodied people would not even attempt—and they don't just begin. They see their vision through to their goal.

It is very likely that most people who find themselves victims of an accident like Rick Hansen's, go through a period of denial and then resentment. The difference is that the visionaries, the doers, are the ones who turn that energy into a worthy cause. They take everything in their situation and mobilize their dreams, creating a reality that takes them further than most of us dare to dream.

Sam Sullivan is a quadriplegic as a result of a skiing accident at nineteen. After recovering from depression, he completed a Bachelor degree in Business Administration, founded six non-profit organizations to help people with disabilities, and became Mayor of the City of Vancouver. He is another example that demonstrates that while an accident may alter one's life, it needs not destroy visions and successes.

Acceptance of Limitations

Society as a whole is caught in a fast-food mentality. We want instant gratification. We want it all and we want it now. It doesn't work that way. Most things that are worth achieving take time. Sometimes it seems like someone rises to stardom or success quickly and easily, making it seem like some people get all the luck. That isn't really true. Anyone who even gets that far has practiced more and sweated harder to achieve their personal goals along the way than is apparent.

Most of our limitations are not financial, physical or mental; The only real limitation we have is time. Time is finite. It is out of our control. We can overcome the limitations we have in the areas of finances. It is a matter of understanding where to start, how to align ourselves, and how to do great things on limited budgets. There are many examples of businesses started by people who have very limited financial resources. In one sense, people who have limited financial means are often more willing to take financial risks as they have less to lose.

So if the person with less to lose will take a bigger risk, this must mean that humans are motivated to inaction when they feel they may lose their security. However, the biggest risk of all is inaction. Inaction is the surest method of losing one's security. If you don't think so, just imagine what would happen if you didn't get out of bed each day to go to work—how long would it take to lose your home? A home is one of our strongest links to security.

Acceptance of Risk

Risk is a given. It is everywhere. The only thing we can do about it is to determine how we manage it. That's right, we can manage risk. Risk management can mean removing unnecessary negative variables. When we exercise our skills in all areas of our personal growth, we become more attuned to how to deal with risk-taking situations.

Take risks, even if they are only small symbolic risks. Our risk taking capacity is like a muscle. The person who has taken no chances is far more reluctant to try something like white water rafting than the person who has engaged in other risk-taking behavior. It isn't difficult for me to take risks in some areas of my life, but I am much more reluctant to take risks in areas where I had negative experiences in the past. Learning to moderate risks in all areas, not taking inappropriate risks or inappropriately avoiding taking risk in other areas is a lifetime challenge.

Acceptance is not surrender. Surrender is waving the white flag. White flags don't go anywhere in the battlefield of personal growth. Acceptance is recognizing what is, what is possible and doing what we can with what we have and learning how to reach out for the help we need. Isolation or going it alone are seldom beneficial when we are seeking to grow. Most things worth doing are too big to do alone. Find a coach. Seek to find comrades. There is strength in numbers.

Retirement Requires Adaptability

Tom, like many businessmen running one-man businesses, worked long days and sacrificed holidays. He owned a Shell Oil Agency fueling tug boats and dredges on the Fraser River. The harder he worked, the more money he made. "I worked 8 to 9 hours a day and was always on call. If the tide was up, the boats came and I had to go fuel them even if it was 1:00 or 2:00AM. When I was 53, I decided I had paid enough tax and wanted to retire and travel," says Tom.

Most people who did not travel extensively during their working years are unlikely to become the next Magellan during their retirement. The same goes for physical fitness and sports. The inactive worker is unlikely to retire and rival Babe Ruth, Lance Armstrong or Wayne Gretsky. Rebirth of a childhood dream may occur; there are the Rocky Balboa's, but launching a dramatically different life requires astronomical commitment and every over-night success takes at least 10 years.

Life circumstances curtailed Tom's opportunity to travel. As I listened to Tom's story, he revealed a retirement that most of us would have difficulty accepting. At age 57 he had a heart attack; another heart attack at 59. Then his wife needed a new hip. Not long after she had the hip replacement, she succumbed to Lou Gehrig's disease. Tom learned to do housework, cook, and be a caregiver for his wife during the five-year decline prior to her death.

His care giving did not end there. In a twist of fate, Tom spent another five years caring for his mother-in-law who had resented him from the day he married her daughter. Few 65-year-old men (or women) would invest the next five years of their lives caring for an in-law who didn't like them. We can hardly call this a dream retirement.

His mother-in-law moved to Canada from England, because Tom had married her only daughter as a war bride and had taken her away to Canada. She constantly interfered with Tom's wife's life, prohibiting her to participate in any clubs, as she argued her marriage would not last and that she would want to return to England.

It seemed as we talked that after the mother-in-law's passing, Tom's life had been easier. He told of his extensive volunteer activities and even as he related his story, not once was there a trace of bitterness over the difficulties life had dealt him. I queried, "Considering you had two heart attacks at 57 and 59 you are doing very well to be healthy and active at 83. What do you attribute your longevity and good health to?" I stood to be corrected.

"In 2014, I suffered a massive heart attack and died. They resuscitated me with paddles. Then they found out I had some other health issues they needed to take care of before they could do open heart surgery. So, I was in the hospital for nine weeks," he responded.

I was so amazed by his attitude. As we sat and talked, other residents walked past us in the lounge, many with looks of despair on their faces. Tom greeted each one and lifted their spirits. Several times he said, "Vancouver General had been such a help to me through my wife's illness. I just wanted to give back. Again, during my mother-in-law's last years, Vancouver General was so good to me. I volunteer because I see so many people that need help. I just want to help them." Tom continues to make a difference in the lives of others.

It is not the circumstances that determine a person's destiny. It is the attitude with which they respond to those circumstances. It is easy to shrink from the challenge. Certified Retirement Coaches are offering programs to help pre-retirees and retired adults to achieve meaning and satisfaction in their retirement.

Typically, a coach helps the retiree understand the life arenas they need to focus on if they want to initiate a meaningful retirement. Pre-retirement coaching gives individuals an opportunity to formulate their own *Retirement Statement of Intent* and to design a *Retirement Life Plan*.

With any plan, there are contingency plans to help you prepare for the unexpected. Some retirees, when faced with experiences like Tom faced, fall off the wagon and can't get back on. Working with a coach before it becomes a necessity is like insuring your emotional well-being.

"If you always do what you always have done, then you will always get what you always have got" applies to retirement lifestyle. However, if you want your retirement years to bring excitement and opportunity, it is possible. It is even possible to rejuvenate the dreams abandoned years before and to live a retirement that includes the best days of your life. Retirement is a lot like an entrepreneurial venture. It requires a tolerance for ambiguity, great flexibility, tenacity and innovation. Creating a meaningful retirement requires the development of a plan and diligence to revise the plan and keep the plan alive.

If you have attended personal development programs and courses or through your work involved with developing a Corporate Mission Statement, it may not seem like such a stretch to apply this to your personal life. If the whole concept of sitting down and planning for success seems foreign, consider these options and tips to help you become a Champion of Change:

Push beyond your comfort zones in one area at a time.

- It takes a consistent long-term effort to develop new habits.
- Written achievable steps increase success when building new habits.
- Develop step-by-step simple rules to aid the process.
- Seeking and finding supportive environments often helps us to make change happen.
- Establish routines where necessary while remaining adaptive.
- Choose to be an agent of change, have self-awareness, volition and intentionality.
- Develop a clear sense of vision and purpose to make self-initiated change easier.
- Monitor your progress and honor your successes.
- Avoid joining groups where leadership ignores or avoids change, because of

members or leaders who are overly controlling.
- Hire a coach to help draw attention to areas of variance between your expectations and behaviors.

You can achieve your dreams in life at any age. Walt Disney's most creative years were the last ten years of his life. Retirement need not be a barrier to your success. With active planning, you can enjoy the best days yet.

CHAPTER 10

CONGRUENCE AND STRATEGY:

CERTAINTY OR PARADOX

It is a paradoxical but profoundly true and important principle of life that the most likely way to reach a goal is to be aiming not at that goal itself but at some more ambitious goal beyond it.

Arnold Toynbee (1889 - 1975)

Nature never intended for us to be chameleons—passively fitting into our surroundings or to live in thoughtless conformity. There is a difference between open-mindedness and lacking the initiative to develop a strong personal identity and value system. People who fail to develop a clear identity lead a miserable retirement. Debilitated by low self-esteem, they drift into apathy. They can stay there and live at zero or they can choose to break free.

The movers and shakers, the people who make a difference in their own lives and the lives of others, are not afraid to stand out. It is through a willingness to move beyond mediocrity that enables us to be most fulfilled. Sometimes it means we need to do things we would rather not do. Personal growth is like physical fitness—no pain—no gain. Self-exploration and evaluating our beliefs can be difficult. However, the personal growth rewards make it well worth the effort.

To break free from mediocrity, we must evaluate what we believe and why. The WHY is the really important part. Values are our beliefs weighted according to the importance we place on one belief over another. If our life isn't bringing us the satisfaction we crave, we need to examine our belief system. Do we attempt to maintain conflicting beliefs? What are they? Are some of these beliefs an attempt to maintain the status quo?

Inconsistencies are frequently wrapped around tentative wording: "I think I probably could," "Sometime I might," "I should try it," and similar phrases. Or in language that absolves us of carrying through: "I think that, but...," "Usually, except when...," or similar language. Words like "but" or "except" cancel the meaning of the first part of the sentence. We contradict ourselves when we say we believe one thing and do another. It may be an attempt to conceal our apprehensions about how others will respond.

It is not possible to operate by different rules in different aspects of our lives, without running into conflict with our own beliefs. It leads to inner turmoil, because we are ignoring values we believe to be important. This leads to remorse or guilt, followed by rationalization. We must take a serious look at the beliefs we operate by, and how we developed them before we can move on. Some of our beliefs may be very healthy, and others may require revision. Revision stems from the word vision. A clear vision is the foundation for passion and excellence.

Incongruence causes a cacophony of emotions. Congruence in all areas of our life creates internal harmony. Taking action, which is consistent with our internal principles, creates a peaceful melody is in tune with our internal well-being and external environment.

Congruency versus Flexibility

Congruency comes from living in accordance with our values. When our actions are congruent with our values, we know inner peace. Inner peace is the highest level of personal fulfilment. It is easier than living with internal conflict. Congruency and flexibility seem on the surface to create a paradox.

Everything in life, including our personal lives, is fluid, in a constant state of flux. Very few things are concrete and there is less stability than many of us wish to accept. This demands flexibility. However, the ability to balance our life-boat on stormy seas, rising tides as well as on still waters seems to be an art and a science. The ability to create consistent results amidst all this chaos, comes from clarity and persistence.

Flexibility and congruency are not in opposition. When values are used to direct choices, there is still room for flexibility unless our value system is too rigid. Perhaps there is no life stage that requires flexibility more than retirement. During retirement years we confront ever changing conditions and sometimes aging, illness and/or financial constraints result in us needing to be willing to be flexible.

Being willing to be flexible enables us to:

- learn and be open to new information

- understand others and our world, setting us free from mediocrity

If we become rigid in our thinking, navigating through change becomes too difficult. Being open to formal and informal education can help us remain flexible. Expose yourself to as much information as you can get. Digest and evaluate the information, rather than accepting everything verbatim. Determine what you are going to accept and what you are going to discard. Openness to learn and willingness to evaluate new information can enable us to abandon faulty beliefs that are holding us back from achieving what we really want.

Our actions are based on our beliefs. Repeated actions develop into habits—a cycle that reinforces the underlying beliefs. When we identify a faulty belief and abandon it, we need to break the habits that reinforce the former belief, otherwise our new belief will continue to leave us feeling conflicted. When we are thinking about it we know what we want. This is a conscious thought process. However, often we act based on sub-conscious thought. To retrain our sub-conscious mind, we must ensure that we store the new belief there.

Three learning strategies can help us move our revised beliefs and values from a conscious desire to the sub-conscious. Our sub-conscious mind stores information based on:

- Seeing – visual learning
- Hearing – auditory learning
- Doing – kinaesthetic learning

This is why writing beliefs, values and goals down is a powerful strategy. Affirmations are an effective way to process information by hearing it. Actions, even if they are symbolic, create an opportunity to store the information – in the deep recesses of the mind, where it will not be lost.

At first, behavioral change requires conscious thought. As it becomes integrated, the new ways of thinking and acting will result in unconscious competence. The new behavior is automatic and needs little or no conscious thought. The number of repetitions required before a new pattern is adopted varies. It is influenced by the frequency, the length of time an old habit was practiced, and the amount of distinction between the two models of behavior.

Open-minded people can disagree, without feeling threatened. This also helps individuals understand their own needs and desires more accurately. Setting goals without analyzing and revising your belief system and values will lead to a future that replicates the past. When your beliefs and values support your intentions and aspirations, you find a source of synergy that propels you toward the future you desire. The ultimate choice is yours; you either live or you exist.

Lack of Direction

We have discussed two factors that hinder progress in achieving personal goals—lack of clear values and lack of congruency between values and actions. The third factor identified as destructive to progress is the lack of direction. It is a chicken-and-egg question. How does one generate action without seeing a goal, yet without generating action is it even possible to see opportunities and a long-term goal? Sometimes an individual is so disoriented that a long-term goal is unthinkable.

Any direction is better than no direction. Think of a car when it is stuck. It doesn't matter that you want to go forward. If you are stuck, sometimes you must let go of your desire to move forward and accept that a short movement backward is actually the first step toward any possibility of moving forward again.

In the 1930s, Ralph Nelson Elliot discovered that social trends and trend reversals form recognizable patterns. Using stock market data as his main research tool, Elliot discovered that the forever fluctuating stock market corresponds to basic harmony found in nature. His Elliot Wave Theory remains one of the most accurate in predicting market trends even today.

The stock market forms wave patterns that vacillate back and forth in a forward direction and based on the length, direction and frequency of the waves, the market moves continuously in one direction as long as regressions are shorter than progressions. If a regression exceeds the length of the last progression, a trend reversal occurs. Investors make decisions that trigger a chain reaction. It is the joint chain reactions that result in a trend. Elliott isolated thirteen wave patterns that result in directional movement. They recur in the markets again and again, although not necessarily repetitive in time or amplitude.

The intriguing part of the Elliott Wave Theory is that the waves repeat themselves within themselves. The waves are decipherable on a yearly chart, on a weekly chart, on a daily chart, an hourly chart, and a minute chart.

This theory is also very applicable to our progress through life and the process of personal growth. It is unrealistic to assume that we must move forward with no regressions. Even when it seems that we are stuck, it is likely we are moving in some direction. The chain reaction generated by decisions we make in one part of our life impact other areas of our lives. When we recognize the power of influence we wield based on the decisions we make, we are able to remove hurdles from our path—whether the hurdle is internal or external.

As we move through life, there are going to be times when we demonstrate rapid growth with small regressions and other times when the movement is more static. If we tend toward high expectations of ourselves, we may fail to recognize the times when we are garnering energy and strength for our next forward movement, and may see it as a negative place to be in life. Sometimes we need to ride out a plateau before the next ascent.

Understanding this as a metaphor for our own personal progress in retirement transition can enable us to recognize that letting go of the sense of urgency can actually free us to be more productive. At age 50, it felt like time was running out. I simply could not accomplish things fast enough to please me. More recently when I figured out that I will probably live another 30 or 40 years, I learned to be less anxious about the amplitude of my success in any given moment and realized, "I can do it—progress sometimes takes time."

Personal Power

Our ability to become our dream comes from understanding that we have personal power to take action. Loss of personal power leads not only to defeat, but also to depression. Choose Life! Every day you either embrace life or choose to move toward death. Every choice you make either extends your life or shortens your life. Are your choices life-embracing or life-threatening?

When Mae first heard this concept discussed, it was a sobering thought for her, and it was a catalyst for change. At the time she was struggling with PTSD and was under the care of a psychologist who focused on all the reasons why, in his opinion, she was not likely to overcome my challenges. He was feeding helplessness.

As a result, everyday Mae was making choices that were slowly closing down my life—mentally, emotionally, physically and spiritually. Although not overtly suicidal—she felt life as she had known it prior to my car accident and PTSD was gone forever. Everything she did and thought every day was leading toward her demise.

"Every day we make a choice to move toward life or toward death," explained David MacIntosh, the co-facilitator of a weekend laughter workshop. He explained someone had told him those words by a counselor after the suicide death of a close friend of his.

Like most people who lose a friend to suicide, David was remorseful and felt he could in some way have prevented the suicide. The counselor explained that suicide is not an event that happens out of the blue; it is the culmination of a series of choices moving closer and closer toward death.

Self-control doesn't require willpower, it requires vision: it is true freedom. Loss of self-control is bondage. We either exercise our personal power or allow external circumstances and forces to overpower us.

If you believe:

- the world around you is corrupt
- there are few, if any, choices

- even if you were given a choice, you'd make the wrong decision

the result is a sense of hopelessness - a depressive state. One option would be to go to the doctor and get a prescription to mask the symptoms—to numb you so you can't feel. While I will not deny some people benefit from pills, I believe they are more often a band-aid than a true solution. Is covering the evidence, removing the cause? Chronic depression is like a slow form of cancer of the soul. It slowly erodes your sense of self-worth and the sense that your life has meaning and value.

I do not want to over-simplify suicide; it is a complex problem with no easy solutions. Many suicides are related to chemical imbalances and abuse of drugs. However, I believe it is prudent to discuss suicide openly.

The primary precursor of suicide is depression—a problem all too prevalent in our society—and retirees are not immune. Sadly, mental health issues remain a topic most people do not want to discuss. Friends and family may withdraw when they are needed most. This can lead to someone who needs help—feeling reluctant to get it and also may make them feel like even more of a failure.

Significantly more seniors commit suicide than young people do. According to US statistics, 12.4% of the population is made up of seniors but they represent 16% of all suicides, while the young represent 14.2% of the population and only comprised 13.3% of suicides. The American Association of Suicidology states that, on average, a suicide impacts 6 other lives.

Of even greater concern, there are 25 attempts for every one suicide. For every suicide attempt, how many more depressed people are there? Across all ages, suicide is the 11th most common cause of death in the US. In Canada, the stats aren't much different. Additionally, according to Stats Canada, men between 45 and 64 are almost 3 times more likely than women to commit suicide, and after age 65 men are almost 6 times as likely to commit suicide.

These stats are alarming and should concern us not only at a personal level. They need our help to help. They need support to re-engage with life. Forego personal agendas: making choices for them further dis-empowers them. Encourage the depressed person to find their own source of life meaning and support every effort they make to re-engage with life.

Breaking down the Barriers

Honesty

The first step in moving forward is to be honest with yourself. Life is a road map full of "y" intersections. Knowing where we are is crucial. Invariably we know which road will lead us in the direction we want to go, however, sometimes short-cuts or the easier way out tempts us.

My son-in-law was recently describing his attempt to go hiking with his one-year-old son. He intended to cross the border. At the time he checked Customs wait times were only 5 minutes. However, as he approached the border, the signs predicted a 40 minute wait.

As he progressed through the line, the lanes split several times. Each time he had the choice of going right or left. He chooses to go left each time. Then not long after making the choice he would notice it was not moving nearly as quickly as the other line. It ended up taking him over an hour to get across the border.

The baby had slept, but now, it was unlikely the baby would tolerate a hike and hiking would put him back at the border during the peak traffic for crossing the border to return home. The window of opportunity had passed. Hiking was not a viable option. He decided he needed to return home without hiking.

We can do that in any area of life. We have choices. Each time we make a choice we are soon confronted with another choice. If we make random choices, we may repeatedly make the wrong choice and it may cause the loss of an opportunity.

If we are staying in situations that keep us from being able to maintain the traction necessary for progress, we need to take another road.

Without honesty, you are not ready to embrace life to the fullest. It is so easy to look at another person and question why they don't see what they are doing, or why can't they get their act together. It is different when we look at our own situation. Honesty with oneself is difficult, but well worth the effort. Honesty allows you to fill the potholes and make the road lead to a smoother journey.

Inventory of Resources

Focus on the 'haves' not the 'lacks'. People who focus on abundance and opportunity are far more successful than people who focus on the negatives. How often have you stored an item, and when the need arises, you purchase the same item because you forgot you already had one?

Look for resources that have multiple uses. We know that they mainly make a hammer for hammering nails; however, a hammer can also remove nails, provide a hard surface for crushing an item against, or as reinforcement for protecting sheet metal when we are using other devices to bend the metal. List retirement resources including financial resources, skills, experience, social support systems, your psychological strengths, the resources in your community, resources within your family, or your business associates.

Give Yourself Credit

I am a firm believer that every person should create their own halo file. A halo file is a place to keep all the accolades one receives in life. Not only does this help you understand who your supporters are; It can help you polish your tarnished self-esteem when you take a tumble.

Make a list of your accomplishments. Some say that people who make a list of the things they want to accomplish in their lifetime and refer to it often, are more likely to achieve their goals. There is an equally beneficial opportunity to listing your accomplishments and reviewing them: you can see just how much you really have accomplished in the past which empowers you to see how much you could accomplish in the future.

Activate Resilience

In 2006 Vancouver, BC was hit with an early heavy snow fall that destroyed hundreds of 50-year-old cherry trees and other trees. Then came a record-breaking windstorm. They estimate more than 10,000 mature trees fell in Stanley Park, causing a clean-up cost that may reach $10 million.

Most astounding were the immense trees ripped from the ground. Root balls loomed 20 feet upward, leaving a gaping hole where the roots once were. I noticed that one of these root balls took with it many smaller trees; trees that now will either die or contort to stretch skyward to gather the sun's rays and shoot roots toward the ground to gather water.

I thought about the trees that stood tall and upright and lacked the flexibility to bend and tolerate the wind. They snapped like popsicle sticks. I noticed how many trees broke because of their vulnerable position in the forest. Most of the downed trees looked strong and healthy; there seemed to be no explanation why they toppled or broke in the storm while others remained.

Mysteriously, nature turned on herself, destroying some of her greatest wonders and beauty. The after-effects of this storm will leave their mark on this protected natural landscape for centuries to come. Nature's resilience and flexibility will regenerate the forest.

Now more than 10 years later new trees are growing but they are no comparison to the grandeur of the trees destroyed by the storm. Some people face crises in their lives that leave permanent scars. The most important thing is to move forward regardless of what comes our way.

Resilience and flexibility are coping skills that help a person during life-challenges. Taking a look at times in your life where resilience or flexibility helped you out of a tough spot can help you identify the actions and attitudes that set you free before. This can enable you to use them again. While we often can't drive our root systems down deeper in the midst of a storm, identifying the areas of our lives where we have strong roots can help us recognize our strengths and abilities.

Sometimes a storm brings an opportunity for new growth, or an opportunity to re-evaluate how we are living our life. As unpleasant as it is, we have to get out of our comfort zone and shore up our assets before they fall victim to the storm. Coping means doing what is necessary, not necessarily what is convenient.

It is important to have many sources of support for the storms that will come your way in your bonus years. It is inevitable that you will experience health issues of a magnitude you have never yet faced. Having friends, supportive relatives, established relationships with health care providers, financial reserves and a plan addressing these issues is an asset to your ability to survive the storm.

Establish relationships in good times and build a firm root system to help you endure. Practice flexibility in all areas of your life. Flexible people fair better when facing difficult storms than people who have less flexibility.

There is a clear link between our need for control and our ability to deal with crisis. We can be ill-equipped to cope with challenging experiences that make us feel out of control. This requires us to recognize that even strengths can be weaknesses when taken to the extreme. A clear understanding of how our attitude impacts our ability to recover from a difficult experience, serious illness or accident can give us the edge.

Our attitude actually affects the physical aspects of life far more than we realize. If you don't agree, just think of where you feel it if you are very fearful. It gives you a stomach ache, or at least butterflies in your stomach, doesn't it? That is the mucous membrane of your stomach reacting to your emotions. Likewise, anger can bring on a headache. A large portion of our physical suffering has an emotional component.

However, there are storms so immense that nothing can prepare us for them. These storms are sudden serious illnesses, accidents, injuries or even serious health issues for our next of kin, our spouses, or our children. There are many philosophies to explain or justify the storms that enter a person's life: fate, the hand of God, an indication of stupidity, or inappropriate risk-taking behavior.

Having experienced six car accidents in my life – all of them caused by the other driver, I have cheated death more than once. I have more often than I care to appreciate, encountered people who say, "Why are you attracting this stuff into your life?"

A man who survived an accident where he had fractured vertebrae in his neck, also opposes that philosophy: he says, "I don't know why people say that. They just don't get it. People who survive life threatening illnesses or accidents are exceptional. If they survive more than one, that is just additional evidence of their tenacity, verve and vitality. Survivors have something that other people don't have. Some people just don't have what it takes to survive even the first accident."

Survivors will agree that recovery is not an easy process. It takes years. It takes hard work. It takes willingness to keep fighting. Survivors cannot be quitters. In order to thrive, one must not only survive. They must rebuild and must look for opportunities to continually improve their situation. Tenacity and willingness to continue even in the face of poor prospects and through endless setbacks is the path to recovery.

Caregivers are more helpful when the victim has a great attitude. While it would be great to be mindful of this, it isn't always easy to be cheerful in the face of danger, fear, pain and suffering. Caregivers can help best when they take the time to understand what has helped this person rebound from previous difficulties.

Attitude of Gratitude and Optimism

Adopting an attitude of gratitude will give you a lot of mileage. It's like using a bag of kitty litter to get your car moving when you're stuck on ice. The bag of kitty litter is just a little, light weight asset that makes a big difference in a frustrating situation. The attitude of gratitude is the same. Even though optimism is not a panacea, it is a powerful trait, well worth exercising. People enjoy the company of optimistic people and optimism enables us to see reasons for gratitude even when the going gets rough.

By retirement, most of us have seen many storms. Like the tall trees in Stanley Park, we have withstood so many storms that we may feel like we are invincible icons of strength. We may look at others who have shattered in a life storm and thought, "I would never be like that. I am strong and capable." However, no matter how well we have fared in difficult circumstances, we all have breaking points.

The human spirit is amazing. Even broken people can have their optimism renewed. They can once again soar—-even having known paths that others will never face. People who have faced serious illness or other crises that cause them to recognize their mortality, operate from a different perspective. As we age we all come to the place where we are more aware of our mortality.

Do your Research

What is it you need to know in order to get moving? It is one thing to know you need to take action but if you don't know what that action is, it is difficult to take action. Do your research and learn what it is you need to know. Boomers are a generation that has seen unprecedented change. We are more likely than previous generations to learn that social systems will not bail us out or give us meaningful, comfortable retirements.

As the general population ages, it is inevitable that additional stresses on medical systems will threaten socialized medicine even for those countries where socialized medical care has been something we have grown accustomed to.

Boomers raised in rural settings can remember out-houses and the lack of running water. Many things that are now seen as the basic necessities of life have become so ingrained in our expectations that we have become a generation of consumers. The pursuit of possessions, in a materialistic society, has gobbled up the money many intended to save for retirement and they now find themselves approaching this stage of life with a lack of financial resources.

However, with every transition there comes a whole new opportunity. For example, this same generation is the first generation of retirees that has had the opportunity to earn money using the internet from the comfort of their own homes.

If you feel trapped because of financial constraints, your homework involves finding resources and alternatives. Too often it is easy to see only a very limited number of alternatives – all of them seeming less than satisfactory. If this is the case, you have not looked at the problem from enough angles or with an open mind. There are always more alternatives than we see.

Our world today has more choices and options than ever before. We live in a diverse global economy, with more knowledge and resources than any other generation. It creates a paradox. On one hand we can be so overwhelmed with possibilities that we can become indecisive, while on the other hand, there can be many resources that we don't even know about because we are so bombarded with information, some of which can turn out to be irrelevant.

Take a look at the timing; the answer at one time may be different than it will be at another time. Those who know they will not have enough financial resources for 30 or more years are well equipped to take action when they are younger and more capable of generating additional income, than if they procrastinate and adopt a *just in time* approach to their financial dilemmas.

Well researched, two-pronged approaches can provide more security than a single-focussed approach. This may mean taking a debt-reduction and budgeting course at the same time as developing another income stream. It may mean diversifying your income stream.

Facts and knowledge are only useful if they are put into action. Research can provide you with the information you need in order to make informed decisions. Once you have the facts to help you, it is about taking the appropriate action. Looking at a road map for weeks and weeks will not get you to the destination. It is possible to get paralysed by analysis.

Good decisions still require a willingness to take some risk. There will always be some unknowns. Accepting unknowns as a reality and being willing to take incremental steps will move you forward.

Break Out of Your Comfort Zone

We develop comfort zones where it is easy to lapse into stagnation. We become so comfortable that we don't exercise our decision-making or risk-taking abilities. Both risk-taking ability and decision-making ability are like muscles. They only develop with use.

Think of someone bouncing on a trampoline. As they bounce higher and higher, the pressure they exert against the trampoline forces them higher into the air. It is fun, it is exercise and the distance of the bounce is controlled by accelerating or decreasing the thrust of each movement. The process of developing new skills continues until enough confidence is acquired to do a mid-air flip. The mid-air flip requires trusting one's abilities and good judgment.

Taking some level of risk keeps the activity interesting and enjoyable. Playing it too safe leads to boredom and taking too many risks can lead to injury. The fundamental rule for exercise is that anything that becomes routine no longer stimulates new muscle growth. The same rule applies to skills development in most sports and life skills. Use it or lose it.

If you feel unsafe and you are being pushed, you will instinctively push back. It threatens your sense of safety and diminishes your sense of self-confidence. Making the decision to take a risk enables you to savor the moment of victory as you experience the thrill of taking that leap of faith.

Cut Clutter, Lighten your Load and Simplify

Although I have cycled for many years, I would never describe myself as an accomplished cyclist. I am more of a casual rider. I joined a group and the first ride was hard.

It was early spring and after a winter of not cycling much, I was anything but fit. It was the first time I had ever ridden on hog fuel, gravel and dirt trails as most of my cycling is done on paved trails. I rode with a back pack, overloaded with in-case-I-need-it supplies.

I was constantly struggling to keep up and falling further and further behind. I even begged the group to go on without me and let me go at my own pace; however they didn't see this as an option. Little did I realize when I signed up for the trip that what they called an easy ride would turn out to be 27 miles of undulating knolls and hollows.

Their strategy for keeping me with the group was even more problematic for me. They would ride ahead at their pace for a mile or two and then stop and wait for me. While they waited, they became rejuvenated and more energetic. When I finally caught up, I would be totally exhausted and in much need of a rest. They would be raring to go – so off we would go.

It wasn't until the 20th mile that one of the men offered to take my back pack. What an amazing load off my shoulders. Later the same year I had the opportunity to ride a very light-weight folding bicycle and again I learned a huge lesson in travelling light.

Most of us carry too much baggage. But it isn't only emotional baggage I am talking about here; it is the highly draining effort of maintaining things we don't need. If we are maintaining second vehicles, excessive living space, too many toys, too many possessions, too many activities, too many high maintenance friends and/or too many things that we really don't need or use,

it makes it too hard for us to move forward. We live in a "stuff" oriented society. We have more toys and belongings than any previous generation, and it isn't much wonder we find it hard to maintain this lifestyle.

It is much like cleaning up your computer; it can get bogged down with a lot of spy-ware and grey ware and files that we aren't even aware of and before we know it, our computer can be nearly choked with every keystroke. Your typing speed doesn't benefit you if the computer cannot process the data it is receiving. Feeling overwhelmed? Stop. Clean up the clutter. Make it easy to move on.

Brainstorming

If your options seem limited, use a proven technique for developing options. Brainstorming - a method originating with Alex Faickney Osborn's book titled ***Applied Imagination***. Brainstorming offers some distinct possibilities for individuals. The key to brainstorming is to separate yourself from the temptation to qualify and evaluate ideas when you generate them, listing all ideas no matter how lame or far out. It allows a person to come up with more ideas.

Theatrical Thinking

At one stage in my life when I was negotiating a difficult transition, I learned that generating ideas which seemed extreme to me, allowed me to break free of my self-limited thinking. I call this Theatrical Thinking.

An actor takes on identities that may differ greatly from his own philosophy, personality traits and life experience. A good actor can do such a convincing job of being the character, that when viewers see the actor in an interview, they are surprised to see the actor differs greatly from the character being portrayed on screen.

The writer and producer define the role and develop the character—the actor fits into it. If we can do this as we explore alternatives for specific situations, it allows us to step out of our typical roles and behaviors to look at things in a new way. Imagine or write the script for the conservative thinker, the extremely liberated thinker, the ultimate risk taker, the intellectual and the creative thinker, and then the analytical thinker.

As we take on each character, trying to imagine the ideas the character would come up with will probably differ greatly from we would come up with in our own character and comfort zone. We can have fun with this. Some options may be bizarre, out-of-character for us and never a fit. It can help us see different perspectives than we would see on our own. It can be an interesting experience to visualize the sequence of events created by our Theatrical Thinking exercise.

Storyboarding

Storyboarding was originally developed by Walt Disney Studios during the early 1930s. Storyboards allow for experimentation with the storyline, enabling the production crew an opportunity to tweak the film to evoke stronger reactions or interest in the viewer. This enables the producer to inter-mingle flashbacks and fast forwards by inserting clips out of chronological order to build suspense and interest. Imagine being able to do that with your Life Plan. Simply use Post-it™ notes on a bulletin board to list and organize your ideas. It is effective as a way to build a strategy for achieving your goals, and to complete projects with less effort and better results.

Mind Mapping

Porphyry of Tyros, a noted philosopher from the 3rd century, probably developed the first mind maps. He graphically visualized the concept categories of Aristotle. Ramon Lull, Tony Buzan, Alfred Korzybski, Robert A. Heinlein and A. E. van Vogt are all credited with the concept of *mind mapping*.

The mind mapping concept starts with a centrally placed a word or phrase with words, ideas, or tasks placed in thought bubbles surrounding the central concept. Visualizing, categorizing, and generating a web of ideas can spawn new ideas and provide a basis for decision making.

As it is more non-linear than most of our traditional problem-solving processes, it enables us to eliminate hurdles we may otherwise perceive. It forms a cognitive map that includes information that we may edit out when we try to solve problems just by thinking or talking them through. During transitions, strategies that move us out of our typical problem solving patterns can prove very effective.

Six Hat Thinking

Edward DeBono, in his popular 1985 book, ***Six Hat Thinking***, theorized that most people only use one or two thinking styles. He implemented *Parallel Thinking*™ as a method of complimenting lateral thinking. His strategy included the use of various colors of hats to generate thoughts based on: Factual, Emotional, Critical, Positive, Creative and Big Picture thinking.

Learning DeBono's strategies and reading his book is a great way to expand your decision-making skills. It is always easier to move forward when you have made a decision. People who commit to their decisions seldom remain in a state of inaction.

Barrier Deconstruction

Barrier deconstruction enables you to move beyond barriers. Think of it as a road blocked by a barricade. It is easy to turn the corner and take the detour, but how do you really know what is beyond the barricade? While this may not be advisable in a purely literal sense, my father frequently ignored *Road Closed* signs.

I guess it was the pioneer in him. Although I can not imagine, Alberta was little more than a homesteading pioneer's frontier when my father immigrated to Canada in the late 1920s. Even when I was a young child, many rural roads in more remote areas had grass growing down the middle of the two worn tire trails. As new improved roads replaced poorer roads, many rural roads became unmaintained for and abandoned.

Some had "Road Closed" or "Bridge Out" signs erected by the townships; others had hand-made signs erected by the locals. My father loved exploring these roads, much like he loved exploring abandoned mines and ghost towns.

Often those roads led to amazing scenery, far more picturesque than the upgraded roads where the trees were cleared and natural undergrowth destroyed. We often stopped to investigate nearly extinct wild flowers or to watch birds and wildlife. Were our lives enriched by travelling beyond the barricades? Yes, most definitely.

Sometimes Dad's adventures led to finding short-cuts. While there can be a danger in taking uncharted paths, there are many times the barriers in our lives are blocking off pathways to success. They are more often blocking off short-cuts to the destination we most want. Take the time to assess why the barrier exists. Is it a barrier you erected yourself? Can removing it make it easier to achieve your dreams?

Rekindle the Fire – Ignite the Passion

Find that spark and fan it! Even the most complacent person has fire within. It is in there somewhere. It may be so nearly extinguished that you feel there is no sense, but an ever blazing forest fire which destroys thousands of acres of forest starts from a single spark. While untamed firc is destructive, I would contend that next to oxygen, water and food, fire are essential.

Fire is raw power. Fire harnessed can power machinery and manufacturing plants, heat homes, cook food, and sterilize. Without fire, our world would be nearly uninhabitable—and probably instead of the world population being over 6 billion, mankind would face extinction.

What has fuelled your fire in the past? What is worth getting fired up about? What has caused the fire of your passion to die out? Every fire needs a source of fuel. Finding that source of fuel—starting with small kindling—is one strategy that will help you get the fire going again. Fires are easier to start in an oxygen rich environment. If you surround yourself with people who are living their lives to the fullest—the fire of their passion is burning vigorously, and they are keeping the fire of their passions stoked.

Take time to allow nature to inspire you. Oxygen is necessary for fire. Oxygen is a by-product of photosynthesis. The chemical equation for photosynthesis is 6H2O + 6CO2 ↑sunlight and chlorophyll ↑ C6H12O6+ 6O2. Six molecules of water plus six molecules of carbon dioxide, in the presence of sunlight and chlorophyll, produce one molecule of sugar plus six molecules of oxygen.

Sugar is a byproduct of photosynthesis—SWEET. It isn't necessary to sugar-coat the benefit of nature—the sweetness is already there. Nature provides an oxygen rich environment and is an abundant source of metaphors and life lessons. Getting outdoors, away from the hustle and bustle of life, can enable you to clear your head and see new alternatives. No matter how hard it is to fan that little spark into a healthy fire, be a Boy Scout and don't give up. Many a person who lives a life filled with passion has experienced times when their fire waned.

Garner Support

People with more than six social supports in their lives seldom need counselling. Isolation is emotionally, physically, and spiritually detrimental to your well-being. People who have support can rebound more quickly from set-backs. The sad reality is that most people only have two very close supportive friends, which is not enough.

Many of the people we refer to as friends are merely acquaintances and many other people we may consider being our friends do more to sabotage our successes than support them. Most of us never learn how to support others. Learning to be our own best friend first and learning to cultivate supportive friends is a skill that takes attention and practice. It may be unrealistic to expect all our support to come from friends. Social support systems, networking organizations and self-help groups can help provide the support we need.

An organization that offers more than you can ever give back and the best deal for the cost is Toastmasters. Most people who attend Toastmasters have no intention of becoming professional public speakers. Toastmasters gives unconditional support and is the often needed opportunity to stand on your own soap box. Speeches are not judged on content. Your point of view is accepted – unconditionally.

This is very validating and does a lot to bolster self-esteem. Everyone who goes through the Toastmasters program and completes at least one designation comes away with communication skills that are an asset to them in their personal and/or business life.

Healthy support networks increase self-confidence, which generates increased drive and self-motivated action. As confidence grows, the need for validation from others becomes less important, self-motivation kicks in, and the ability to take action in your personal life increases.

Step Away

In those moments when we are blinded by frustration or unsure where to turn, and nothing seems to work, we wonder if we will ever be what we once were or what we dreamed of being. It can become all-consuming. Every waking moment we search for answers and feel like there are none. We wrap ourselves up in the problem and are blinded to the solution. Albert Einstein said, "We can never solve our significant problems from the same level of thinking we were at when we created the problems."

It is time to step away and get a fresh perspective. Physically step away. Go to the beach. Take a brief holiday or do something that is such a diversion from the ordinary that it consumes your thoughts, enables you to break recurring unhelpful thought patterns.

Take a three-day getaway. It can be easier to come up with the answer when we stop thinking about it. Forward action is not always constant; remember the Elliott Wave Theory.

Examine your Self-Talk

We all engage in self-talk at a speed that far exceeds our conscious talk. Evict the critical nag, if you have one renting space in your thoughts. Successful people engage in self-talk that is more like a nurturing parent who supports when support is needed, guides when guidance is needed, praises when praise is needed and encourages when encouragement is needed.

Some people are more internally motivated, while others are more externally motivated. If we allow negative self-talk, we become increasingly dependent on getting validation from external sources and as other people may have their own agenda, this can be problematic. It is far better to recognize your tendency to engage in negative self-talk and work on changing that internal dialogue.

Humor can enable us to shift our perspective, or it can help us recognize that no matter how difficult the present moment is, someday you will be able to look back on this day or situation and laugh at it. Sometimes our awareness of our own behavior becomes clouded. Treat yourself at least as well as you would treat your best friend – you are the best friend you can ever have.

Keep Yourself in the Game

Diversification of interests and activities also serves to keep you energized. If we are dependent on one source of activity, whether it is a job, a hobby, a social group or a volunteer opportunity, and it disappears, it will affect us more than if we have other activities to keep us vital.

Continuing to explore your next move is at least keeping you in the game. If you have stopped exercising completely, starting with slow warm-up exercises prepares you for your next move. If you have become frozen by indecision, making the decision that you are no longer satisfied with your present lifestyle is taking action. Exploring choices is action. Rectifying a mistake you made, is action.

Back to the analogy of the Elliott Wave Theory and the stock market, only a fool looks at a one-minute chart and invests in a flat market assuming that it is necessarily going to move in a given direction.

When the market is going sideways, financial analysts refer to it as consolidation.

Consolidation is where the market builds energy that will eventually result in momentum in one direction or the other. Even very knowledgeable investors using all the calculators used for predicting changes in trend direction cannot guarantee which direction the market is going to move when it takes off again.

There are times when waiting a bit before making your next move is the right choice. It is necessary to be honest. Is waiting only procrastination, or is it a choice in a well-defined strategy?

Step at a Time - Divide and Conquer

Anything complex enough to overwhelm a person is usually a result of several problems. Your ability to resolve complex issues depends in part on your ability to divide the challenges into smaller problems and solve one or two at a time in a systematic way. Difficult tasks can become easy when divided into manageable tasks.

Try it Out

The decision to do something new can get hung up on fear of the unknown or inability to choose from the vast numbers of opportunities available. Try it out! It is much like trying on shoes. What looks great in the shoe store window may look or feel different and may not be comfortable to walk in.

There are careers, jobs, hobbies, business ideas that may seem like the ideal opportunity, but we really don't know for sure until we get involved. Discuss the pros and cons with someone who is already doing it. This has become so easy now with the internet. Contacting someone who is not local can enable you to learn about a particular business opportunity; local people may regard you as a threat if you ask about their business.

Maybe you will try something out and later find it isn't a good fit. As long as it did not require a large up-front investment, not that big of a set-back to regroup and try something different. Many times you just don't know until you try.

Indulge Yourself

Even as you would periodically treat a special friend or loved one, you need to treat you. Giving yourself a reward, such as a trip to an art gallery, a mid-day movie or even a massage can change your environment and enable you to garner the energy to jumpstart your next project. Learn to reward your actions—not your failures.

It's counterproductive to say, "I have had a tough day; I need a double hot fudge sundae." This I can tell you from experience has negative side effects. Far more productive is to purchase myself a rose for exercising 4 times in a week.

Do Something for Someone Else

When we get consumed by our own problems, we cannot see the forest for the trees. When we open our hands, eyes, and heart not just because we think we should show charity, but out of an attitude of service to others, we see things differently.

It is not difficult to find others who are in greater need than ourselves—no matter how difficult things are for us in this moment. Seeing the need of others can help us to become more realistic about our own situation. Choose an opportunity that suits your interests and temperament.

Help children—who can be so carefree and eager to learn. Help elders who have so many rich stories. Helping others enables you to find an opportunity to be of service in an environment that gives you a sense of satisfaction, and inspiration.

Shift from Results Oriented to Process Oriented

We live in a generation of instant gratification - the McD – DQ Syndrome. We want it all, right now! We want more for less and for 79 cents we can upsize it. We honor our wants, rather than our needs. In our lives we substitute quick fixes for what we really want. Quick fixes lead to temporary satisfaction – followed by disappointment. If we learn to enjoy the process, the results are more satisfying and enduring.

Recently I have become much more accepting of my age and more satisfied with where I am no. I have adopted a new habit. I am exercising my appreciation for the small things in life.

They are only small because we expect them. Good meals, freedom, peace, good health, are not small at all. At the end of each day, when I lay down to sleep, I think of all the things I enjoyed during the day and give myself credit for my accomplishments. I end by thinking, “I lived this day well.”

Some people advise living every day as if it was your last. I don’t like that philosophy. If I knew a day was my last, I would round up my family and go to the beach, have a great time enjoying the outdoors, and then go out to dinner together at a lavish restaurant. Obviously, I cannot do that every day. Instead of living every day like it was your last—live every day as your best. Put into that day the best you can in every aspect—attitude being a big part of it. Face each day with the best attitude.

Create an Opportunity

Good advice came from comedian Milton Berle: “If opportunity doesn’t knock, build it a door.” Every time I sit by the ocean at sunset and watch the ships heading out into open waters, I ponder, “Who is on that ship? Where are they going? And, how many people are sitting on the shore, thinking, 'When will my ship come in'?"

Although it is difficult to understand why whales beach themselves, one may wonder if it is in part because the waters have become too polluted or they have somehow lost connection with the innate sense of their need to be far out swimming in the ocean.

We become figuratively beached when we become dissatisfied with the 'pond we are swimming in' or we lose our sense of bearing. We lose connection with the things that give our lives meaning. Opportunities present themselves when we invite them into our lives. Being open, having our eyes open, an open heart and open mind enables us to see beyond the present into an ocean of opportunities.

Work with a Coach

Coaching works! Even successful people do even better when they work with a coach. A coach provides a non-biased sounding board and an accountability partner. If you continue trying to move forward without the help of a coach, you may still be where you are today three or six months from now.

I have had individuals who were reluctant to invest in coaching–they may have attended a workshop I facilitated and got a lot out of it. They may remark, "You are so inspirational, supportive and knowledgeable" or "I learned so much from being here—I wish I would have done this sooner."

Yet, when it comes to one-on-one coaching, they will balk at the expense. Six months may lapse and then they will come and want to arrange one-on-one coaching—and they often express regret that they didn't invest in private coaching sooner. There is nothing more powerful than making the commitment to invest in yourself.

Time spent making poor progress is far more costly than the investment in coaching—even with the most expensive coach. Most coaches charge $100—$150 per hour. It is a fee comparable to any other professional service. The benefits are very personal—so it is an investment in self—you are worth it.

Small adjustments to our thinking add up to big results. Not only from the well-being and peace-of-mind point of view, but also from the financial point of view, coaching is a worthwhile investment. So many people are reluctant to pay for career coaching, yet they are losing money every day staying in a dead-end job or being unemployed. How much is your well-being worth? Are you ready to invest in yourself?

CHAPTER 11

WHAT IS ENOUGH?

SUSTAINABILITY

There is never enough time,

unless you're serving it.

Malcolm Forbes (1919 - 1990)

Those who have worked their whole lives in traditional occupations, managed their money and investments well, have not fallen victim to an expensive divorce, extended periods of unemployment or illness or suffered a business loss are the fortunate few. They are significantly better off than any previous generation and feel quite optimistic about their impending retirement. They have high expectations of living the *good life* and expect a life filled with luxuries and leisure.

Unfortunately, not all have been unscathed by difficulties affecting their financial well-being and health. For them the prospect of retirement isn't so rosy. As discussed earlier, according to EBRI it would seem obvious less than 41% of Boomers feel they have enough money to retire.

Contributing Factors

Divorce, illness or unexpected unemployment erodes our financial status, making the thought of retirement savings vanish from our budgets. For those who have held low-income or seasonal jobs, saving 10% of every paycheck is just not an option. Ask a single parent who raised children without child support, or other single-parent families whether they could squeeze by on 90% of their take-home pay and there will be a resounding—never!

Daryl was only 18, and already the father of two boys when his first divorce occurred. After a second divorce at 26, his second wife took the child of that marriage and moved out of the state. He filed and won custody of his two sons from the first marriage and raised them before marrying again at 42, and having a fourth child with his third wife, only to find himself divorced again a year after the baby was born.

Daryl started paying child support at 18 and didn't make his last child support payment until he was 66. Between age 28 and 36 he had custody of his two sons, however he did not receive child support from his ex-wife. He has no savings for retirement, no employer pensions, and no property. Countless single mothers are in the same situation.

Darlene and her husband, Nathan, were well on their way to the retirement of their dreams, when their son, who had a low-paying job, moved back home at age 27 after his divorce, as he could not manage the financial responsibilities of paying child support and rent for a place of his own.

Unfortunately, 10 years later, his financial status has not improved. Fed-up with having him living with them, Darlene and Nathan purchased a fifth wheel, which they have parked in their yard for their son to live in.

Now 60, Darlene worries about retiring. Already she spends her weekends cooking and doing things for her son and her two grandchildren now aged 11 and 13. She is concerned that she will become a full-time caregiver if she retires, as her son wants the full-time custody of the children.

This impacts not only Darlene and Nathan's retirement but also calls into question how prepared will their son be when he reaches retirement? When is helping not helping? How do you stop a ripple effect?

Marc, whose net worth had been several million, had traveled and lived a great retirement lifestyle until a hefty investment in Bre-Ex gold mining stocks caught him in a fiasco that caused him and many others to lose most of their life savings. Now at 74, he was left with only enough money to live a frugal lifestyle for another 3 years. He was hoping to buoy up his resources by seeking a well-paying full-time job while his health was still good—expecting that he may live 10 to 15 more years.

Besides physical suffering because of accidents or critical illness, even if the crisis resolves itself, it can clean out the bank account. In Canada, with access to government health care, other factors such as extended lost time off work or time taken off work to be with an ill loved one, can add up to 10s or even 100s of thousands of dollars of financial loss. The assumption that insurance covers these losses is often erroneous.

We can't rely on traditional pension plans upon. Employer-paid pensions are almost non-existent, in anything other than union jobs or government jobs. Financial planners admonish the Late-Bloomer-Boomers who have not yet established a hefty retirement savings portfolio to get with it and save every penny.

With life expectancy getting longer and cost of living higher, small and frugal spending alone will not fill the gap. In theory, saving for the future is easy. In reality—given a few rough breaks, it can be nearly impossible. Not that there aren't many people who have habits and lifestyles that cause their predicament. For them learning to spend less and save more is merely a life skill they must learn.

During retirement, with more available time—it can be even easier to overspend and the opportunities for income generation can continue to dry up. Next comes the question of where to invest. The fewer the number of income-generating years you have, and the more limited your resources, the less room you have for risk. Risky investments are a pitfall the size of the Grand Canyon for some retirees.

Many people need the assistance of a good Succession Planner and tax strategist to identify tax exempt ways to remove money from Registered Retirement Savings Plans in Canada or 401K's in the US. Sometimes the strategies need to start long before retirement. Probably at least 10 years before. However, taking the time to learn financial strategies is well-advised. Remember that most financial planners are motivated by the commissions they get for selling products. Aggressive marketing campaigns may cause financial planners promoting a product that is not in your best interests.

Many Canadians feel a sense of panic over the possibility of the government not being able to sustain the Old Age Pension or Canada Pension Plan. However, there is a huge resource resting in the hands of the government: all the billions of dollars people have stashed in Registered Retirement Savings Plans. That money is normally taxable upon retirement—when you withdraw it.

While the assumption is that your income is lower during retirement and therefore you are paying tax at a lower rate, your nest egg is also the government's nest egg. Unless you work with a good tax strategist, more will be in the hands of the government and less in your hands than you ever thought. Even saving for retirement is challenged by low interest rates that make saving seem hopeless. Reverse mortgages or moving to areas with lower-priced properties or moving into a smaller home in order to cut the cost of living may provide some relief.

However, for someone with little or no savings, that may mean a cabin in the bush of northern Canada—appealing to some, but unthinkable for others. With the rising prices of real estate, one has to be well-heeled to buy even a cabin anywhere with a view, water, or amenities. A new trend toward co-habiting, a rerun of the hippie generation communal living, is emerging where singles or married people may live in shared accommodation. It may accommodate 4 to 20 adults who share main living areas and have large bedroom-ensuite combinations.
.

Sustainable retirement may mean having a vegetable garden, using energy sources that are low cost and thinking twice about money spent to purchase a new, or newer vehicle. It definitely dictates getting rid of the gas guzzling SUV—but there are more reasons for getting rid of the SUV than just financial.

Bartering for services, and seniors helping one another are other assets for aging populations on limited budgets. Relationships are crucial to being able to remain healthy and independent in the senior years. Building relationships with people who can help you through mutual exchange and/or support protects you from loneliness and isolation, leaving you less vulnerable. Become a recycling guru. Replacing or remodeling your home may not mean huge expense. There are many opportunities for gathering recycled building products.

For example, as building codes move toward stricter environmental standards in larger cities, it forces some apartment managers to replace every toilet with a low-flush model. If you live in a rural area and need to replace a toilet, a used toilet may be free or almost free. In fact, it is quite in vogue to build using recycled cupboard doors, doorknobs and so on—creating a retro look.

Build a lifestyle and a community that will provide you with your basic needs and create a low-maintenance existence for yourself. It may involve an investment of time and energy—while you are still capable—to build a support system around you that will exist when your needs exceed your abilities.

There are places where prices are very low compared to larger cities. A small handyman's special in Vancouver, BC would cost about $1,500,000 whereas in dying farm towns in rural Alberta, an 1100 square foot house in a similar condition would cost approximately $100,000.

The same is true in the US. If you choose to live near Laguna Beach, California you will be considering properties approaching the million dollar mark. I found a website with stories of houses under $50,000. The website featured a fixer-upper in rural Montana purchased for $17,000. Those are the extremes. There are many options in between.

Relocating may not be an option. Family is important and leaving a lifetime of friends and memories is not only unappealing–it can be terrifying. It all depends on your sense of adventure. If you have lived rurally all your life but want to leave life on the farm, small college towns usually have a vibrant atmosphere interspersed with an active retirement community.

Seniors have been trendsetters throughout their lives and it will be the same as they move into the Segue Years. Politically, sociologically, appetite for cultural events, viewing or participating in sports, shopping and traveling habits and every other behavior that defines them differ from individual to individual and from couple to couple. *The norm* may just be an illusion created by demographers who have their keen need to define things numerically.

Individual needs and values vary. If this is the generation described as more affluent and more educated than any previous generation—we may need to go one step further and state this is the most diverse generation ever, to reach retirement.

Necessity has always been the mother of invention. Even from early windmills that generated a source of power, we see a return too much more sophisticated wind-driven power generation plants. It is self-limiting to assume that Boomers will struggle to find their way through retirement years. They are a creative, innovative generation, well adapted to constant and rapid change. We cannot even predict the unique ways of living and coping that they will develop over the next twenty to thirty years.

The creative ingenuity of the Boomers will give a future to Boom-towns, Boom-housing, Boom-businesses and Boom-clubs. For some retirees, there is a need for supplemental income to fund their lifestyle or their later years. The ability to do something they will love and that will provide meaning to their lives is crucial to a happy and healthy retirement. Nevertheless, the decision whether this needs to come from a secondary part-time job or from a business startup is not always easy.

CHAPTER 12

LIVE LIKE A MILLIONAIRE:

LIVING A RICH RETIREMENT

Develop interest in life as you see it; in people, things, literature, music – the world is so rich, simply throbbing with rich treasures, beautiful souls and interesting people. Forget yourself.

Henry Miller (1891 – 1980)

Immediately, when you think of riches, you think of financial riches. However, there are people who are financially rich and impoverished in every other sense. Ranging from the spending habits of people who are millionaires to other practical ideas of how to experience an emotionally enriching life, being a millionaire at least in some sense is within the reach of all of us.

Taking a serious look at the financial picture for our last 30 to 40 years of life is not only prudent, it is necessary. We are living longer. Pensions do not sustain us. We need a plan.

Spend like a Millionaire

Many millionaires earned more money than people at the other end of the financial spectrum. Others who attain a net worth in the millions earned mediocre salaries. They get there because they did not squander money. Money management and debt-free living are the keys to being financially better off.

Many people buy homes utilizing the biggest mortgage they can obtain. This is not a good plan. The home you live in is not really an investment. While the value may accrue, living in a home with a smaller mortgage enables you to diversify your investments.

Ensuring you can invest the top 10% of your income and then pay your mortgage and lifestyle expenses is much wiser than attempting to save 10% after all expenses. We all know the last thing on our list is the one we give up first. If saving is last on our list, we will repeatedly make excuses why we can't do it this month.

For many readers talking about a discussion about mortgage payments comes a little late. However, it is also a source of concern if you are still paying mortgage payments at the stage of life where you are qualified to collect pensions. We cannot sustain mortgage payments on pensions. The money to pay the mortgage comes either from savings or from continuing to earn income. At some point, there needs to be a reality check.

Live within your means. Spending on credit cards without paying off the monthly balance makes the bank wealthy. Paying credit card interest is the ticket to poverty. For many years, interest on savings accounts has stayed below 3%. Yet credit card interest rates have remained at 18 to 21%.

It takes 30 years to pay off a $2,000 credit balance with an 18% annual rate if you the minimum monthly payment (usually 2% of the balance). During that time, you would end up paying more $4,931 in interest and charges, 146% more than the original balance on the card, according to an online calculator on credit-card comparison site, CreditCards.com.

Credit card debt can drown anyone who relies on pensions for their primary living expenses. Sometimes people delude themselves into seeing government paid pensions as free money. They disassociate the connection between money coming into the home, from money going out.

Any money spent on a credit card that you cannot pay off in full when you get your statement is money spent prematurely. It represents a failure to accept delayed gratification. It is living in the illusion that you can afford more than you actually can.

While there is some legitimacy to using a credit car to do a major car repair or to address some unexpected expense, prudent money management dictates that even then you should manage your finances in a way that you have a contingency fund to cover unexpected expenses.

In 2019, The Financial Times (UK) and Forbes magazine both reported the startling trend in bankruptcy among seniors. An Indiana Legal studies research reported that in 1991, elders made up 2% of the bankruptcy relief claims; by 2019, the share increased to 12%.

Their research also showed 78% of elder households that filed for bankruptcy in 2016 made less than median total income.

It is no secret that health can play into financial strain for seniors. In the US where health costs leave people more vulnerable, it is far worse than in Canada where most health care costs are covered.

However, even in Canada there are a good deal of health-related expenses that are not covered. Hearing aids, visual aids and therapies and dental costs are not covered. Additional needs like chiropractic, massage or other therapies necessary for people with mobility issues are not covered—or are minimally and inadequately covered for the lowest income seniors.

Laura, a Canadian, has asthma and has no need for an inhaler if she takes a herbal tonic that costs $49 a month. Additionally, she needs hearing aid batteries, regular physiotherapy or massage therapy, and requires glasses and eye therapies. Her uncovered health costs per annum amount to $3,600. She was disabled and unable to work past 50. Now on pensions, without savings, these costs are difficult to cover. Government pensions at best amount to only a few dollars a month more than the poverty line.

Laura is a senior living alone and renting. She relies on food from food banks. This is only one example.

Meredith works full time so she and her husband can benefit from employer paid extended health insurance benefits. Most employers supply extended health insurance benefits to their employees. While individuals can buy extended health benefit insurance, it is cost prohibitive and beyond the means of seniors who rely on pensions and do not have retirement savings.

Her husband has complex health problems. They could not cover the cost of his needs. The low paid big box retail job Meredith does is difficult for her. However, she felt she had no choice.

Therefore, the reason more seniors are working past 65, or even well into their 70s is not always a matter of them being bored or unfulfilled. It is a need. Whether it is a need or a desire for greater fulfillment, the key point remains—can one design a plan that works?

Designing a second-wind career, or business endeavor that enables them to have life balance, do something they enjoy and maintain their own health and well-being needs is often a complex challenge. Managing on limited income takes ingenuity, thoughtful consideration and wise decisions.

Work from the Inside Out

Inner peace is a valuable treasure. If you have it and maintain it; age will not deter it, poverty will not diminish it and other people, while they may impact you in the short-term, cannot destroy your inner being. It is your gift to yourself that keeps on giving.

Inner peace dispels violence, hatred, prejudice and judgment. Learning to have a mind open to possibility, unburdened by attachment to things we cannot change and filled with optimism enables you to be emotionally free.

Invest in Emotional Riches

Becoming attached to outcomes or to the past can destroy emotional wealth. Patience enables you to push through difficult circumstances knowing all is going to be okay. Exercise your *Emotional Intelligence* and learn to use your emotions to your advantage. Strong positive emotion attached to empowering beliefs brings consistent results. Keep your word. Be dependable and live without regrets; This leads to a better feeling about oneself and ensures emotional well-being.

Maintain an Income

Millionaires have a perpetual income generated from their investments. If you do not have enough perpetual income to enable you to manage your retirement without financial stress, consider earning an income. Explore opportunities that continue to generate income in the years immediately following your departure from your full-time career. People who retire to working at something they love, enjoy their lives more and find fulfillment whether they are earning the money they need to extend their retirement savings or volunteering. This is the best way to invest in your future financial well-being.

Invest in Spiritual Wealth

Transcending personal challenges and celebrating the real meaning of existence, however we understand the universe or our connections to spirituality, is life transforming. When you start living for what is really important to you, your dreams shift to become a reality. What we give the most energy to—fills our life.

Blatant self-indulgence isn't the real ticket to happiness—the innate desire to be a contributor results in greater happiness when we learn to balance contribution, leisure, our own well-being and financial needs. It is the ability to see beyond ourselves and embrace the big picture that enables us to feel fulfilled. Manifest gratitude. Celebrate your spirituality—connect with God or exercise your own spiritual connectedness.

Take a Risk

Risk taking can lead to enrichment and gratification. Let your song emerge—paint the world red, if that is who you arc. Open minds explore, are curious and see opportunities where the closed mind sees only problems.

While the analytical left side of your brain wants concrete answers, the right brain is creative. The right side of your brain wants to experience things outside the box. It begs you to take the risk of finding out who you really are and it is the music within you waiting to fill the world with singing. Unless you celebrate who you are and what you are, neither you nor the world will experience your true potential.

Be Authentic

Being authentic allows you to experience love, harmony, kindness, peace, and joy. If you have these traits, it will attract other authentic people to you. You must have it yourself before you can give it to others.

When we find our purpose, we can be of service to others. We will no longer feel like we are in pursuit of things we cannot attain. You will enjoy silence and serenity. As long as you define your life by accomplishments and possessions, you cannot know the inner quietness that comes from being in harmony with your life purpose. Meditation is one avenue that enables you to feel connected to the spiritual peace that comes from inner congruence.

Focus on Strengths

Your strengths are the currency in your bank account of personal power. Avoid all thoughts that lead toward weakness and embrace your strength and resilience to become who you really are. Apathy, fear and anger are crippling mentalities that will sabotage even the strongest attempts to mow through the sludge of negativity they create. Explore the dynamic and rich variety of choices that lay waiting for you. You have options and you can make a wide variety of choices that lead to a lifestyle that is satisfying and fulfilling at this stage of life.

Best Kept Secret

Sports provide camaraderie, a sense of achievement, physical well-being, and purpose. For many seniors, sports are a life-enriching experience. For June, her involvement with BC Seniors Games started in 1991 when she turned 55, and a friend encouraged her to participate in the Golf *try outs* for the games. "On being called to tee, we shook hands and wished each other a good game. By this time my stomach was churning! And my first ball went straight into the water! So much for a good start! As we progressed, I began to settle down and get more confident and enjoy the company."

June compares the BC Seniors Games to a mini-Olympics and each year, communities across the province bid to host the games. The games include 3000 to 3500 participating seniors annually. Membership stands at about 5000. The camaraderie and opportunity to stay fit draws participants from communities all over the province. In fact, "Prince George has a higher level of participation based on the percentage of their population, than do the larger cities," relates June.

Organizing the games is an immense amount of work. Members of the Executive Committee commit to 4 hours a day for many months. The organization lacks funding. The largest sponsor is the Legion which contributes $15,000; that covers the medals. Other than that, there are only a handful of corporate sponsors who contribute smaller amounts."

June was a nurse and retired early due to health problems when she was only 47. "At that time I felt I could die. You really want to think you are invincible, and I didn't realize how close I came to not making it at that time. Now every day I wake up and say, 'Thank you.' Every day that I wake up above the greens is a good day. My advice to people approaching retirement is to have a positive attitude and enjoy life."

For anyone who is going through the challenges of health problems, June is an inspiration. She is now 72 and enjoying life to the full – a picture that is quite different from what it was for her at 47. June self-describes as a "tomboy when I was growing up. I loved to play soccer. I grew up in Wales. I also played tennis for a few years after I retired, but due to a back problem I had to give it up. Even to play golf, I need a cart. I cannot stand around for long periods of time."

Her advice to retirees: "Think about the 8 hours a day you spent working. How are you going to fill that? What is it you are interested in? Maybe for some it is a business. For others it may be getting involved in sports. For others it is church activities. Whatever it takes to give them satisfaction that is what they should do. Having less time at the end of the day with nothing to do and ending the day feeling you have achieved something makes retirement worth living."

Keeping Active

According to StatsCan, BC seniors are more active than seniors in other provinces. 51.2 percent of those 65 and over in B.C. are either physically active or moderately active. The national average is 41.4 percent. Other provinces like Manitoba (34.7 percent) and Newfoundland (28.9 percent) are less active.

Dan, aged 78 and a resident of Sidney, BC, spends about 10 hours per week training for the decathlon — lifting weights, distance running and practicing everything from javelin to high jump — despite enduring quadruple bypass surgery two years ago. He entered the World Masters Championship for mature athletes in Italy.

John started his involvement with BC Seniors Games after his retirement at age 55 from the former Woodward's Stores. After the store closed, they hired him back on contract for a while but needed something to do and got involved with slo-pitch. He also joined a Senior's Tennis Club.

He practices almost daily. In 1992 he became the Director of the BC Seniors Games for Zone 4. Then he was VP, then President and now is Past

President. Involvement in the administration of the games was a great way to stay mentally active and a great way to meet people.

His involvement in the community stretches beyond slo-pitch and Tennis. He is involved with the North Shore Safety Council, Woodward's Retirees Association and is helping a man who has Cystic Fibrosis and lost his grant for care. He and another man help him with individual care as part of their volunteer duties with a client support group. As Vice President of the North Shore Optimist Club he helps raise money for kids' sports and to raise funds to assist parents who have to stay in Vancouver to be near their child undergoing cancer treatment at the BC Children's Hospital.

He plays tennis from 6:45 to 9:00AM Tuesday and Thursday and exercises from 9:00 to 10:00AM. He also plays tennis on Monday, Wednesday and Friday. It is easy to assume this active man hasn't faced physical struggles or set-backs—set-backs that many people never get back up from. However, he had a hip replacement a few years ago. It only kept him out of the game for a year. He now enjoys gardening with his wife in his spare time.

"The biggest payoff is that I am healthier, I don't tire easily, because I am fit. I can't sit still and watch TV. Being active keeps you healthy." John shares, "I get meaning from giving back to the community. It provides personal satisfaction. I look at my children and their spouses. They are busy working and raising families. They do not have the time to join service clubs. Seniors have the opportunity to contribute in this way—a way that isn't possible for people who are busy earning a living and raising a family."

"BC Seniors Games is a catalyst for most people who are members. However, most of them are doing it because they played when they were kids in school and now they have the time to get back to it." During his career, he transferred often, and it was difficult to build a social network. Being involved with sports gives him an opportunity to build tremendous friendships.

John provides us a model of a balanced life. He is involved with gardening with his wife, involved in community service organizations generating funds for worthy causes, he is physically active in sports and socially active with his sporting friends. He doesn't have a problem with boredom or lack of purpose. Through sports these seniors live a rich life

CHAPTER 13

IN CHARGE:

BE YOUR OWN BOSS

Life grants nothing to us mortals
without hard work.

Horace (65 BCE - 8 BCE), Satires

What about self-employment and business ownership? Many studies indicate increasing numbers of people are opting for self-employment or business ownership income sources. Self-employment provides yourself a job. Self-employment typically involves providing a service and getting paid for it directly by the end-user rather than through a third party such as an employer.

Business ownership on the other hand is building an entity with the intention of being able to sell the business at a later date or with the intent of other people (employees) doing the work. While business owners may or may not work at the business, many of them hope that at some point, business ownership will grant them income and time freedom. Self-employment and business ownership have their own challenges and implications. Let's look at these individually:

Self-Employment

A civil engineer working in a building permits department, was nearing his eligibility for early retirement. He became increasingly dissatisfied due to bureaucratic and political decisions beyond his control. He decided to start his own home inspection business. It provided more freedom, enabled him to use transferable skills and required little financial outlay.

The main downside of self-employment in the later half of life is the risk. Everything rests squarely on your shoulders. You are the business decision maker and the decisions you make either ensure or threaten the success of the company.

Can you handle peak rush times without working 50 – 60 hours a week? Will you be able to maintain life balance? A lot of people go into self-employment assuming it gives time freedom, but find it gives the reverse – you are not able to go home at night leaving the boss to tie up loose ends. It is almost a given that at some point a surgery, illness or accident will interrupt your ability to work. It doesn't even have to be a crisis in your own life; it can be a crisis in the life of a family member or loved one. What about spouses, aging parents or adult children?

The decision about self-employment needs to be made with careful consideration of these issues, and the availability of disability insurance should be considered. The interesting challenge is that most often you can't qualify for disability insurance without proving your business success first.

Also, most disability insurance will not cover pre-existing illnesses. Read the fine print, and don't underestimate the power of insurance companies to argue that the stomach ache you visited the doctor with three years ago, was really misdiagnosed and that a critical illness was already preexisting prior to the date you took out the policy.

All of this is not intended to cast doubt on the viability of self-employment. Self-employment is a very viable option. Be prepared; work with a coach and ensure you have clearly laid out a plan. Have you chosen a good opportunity or are you doing something because you feel you have no other choice? Is it sustainable, and how long will it take for it to turn a profit? How easy is it to access your target market? Can your nest egg withstand start-up or the possibility that your venture will not get off the ground?

Business Ownership

Bhupinder was ready to retire from his job with the National Food Inspection Agency. His love for his native foods, and knowledge of the food services industry led to a decision to start a manufacturing business, bringing spice mixes and heat-and-serve South Asian cuisine to major grocery store chains. It seemed like a great plan. He had a large extended family that was interested in helping out in the business. Start-up cost ended up being more than 6 times what Bhupinder expected.

He borrowed heavily from banks, and gathered angel money (money loaned by loved ones). Bhupinder was prepared to work long hours at first, however the business took off quickly and he found himself working harder than ever. It wasn't possible to cut back his hours. His financial risk was high and the worry about the business consumed both his waking and sleeping hours.

Soon the business hit a hiccup; they needed more equipment and already everyone except Bhupinder was drawing a salary. For all his hard work he had nothing to show for it other than bags under his eyes and a debt-ratio that threatened his entire retirement savings. Even though business was brisk, financing and start-up costs meant it could take another three years to determine whether the business would ever make a profit, let alone wages for Bhupinder.

Having the foresight to see how business risk could impact your future financial security is difficult. No one goes into business intending to fail. In fact, people who invest money in business, at some level, must be optimistic. A pessimistic attitude will never work in a business start-up situation.

During the past ten years the fastest growing demographic in business ownership has been women. Studies predict that seniors are now taking over as the fastest growing demographic to go into business for themselves. It is expected that seniors will continue to lead the way for new business ownerships.

For some people this comes from a life-long itch to be in business for oneself. For others it comes as a necessity, through retirement coming before they are financially ready. Other times, it results from trying to find meaning once they recognize that clicking the remote or chasing a little white ball around a huge green lawn day-after-day fails to provide meaning.

Business ownership is a lot of responsibility. However, the scariest part is that many retirees consider investing part of their nest egg or the equity from their home into an unproven venture. Along with unproven ventures, I include buying out existing businesses or franchises. Just because franchises have proven systems, it is not a fail proof indication that you will be successful.

Although some franchises turn out to be million dollar ventures, there are many where the owners work 80 hours a week and still barely stay afloat. Retail fast food businesses, where you are dependent on large numbers of part-time, low paid employees are among the toughest businesses of all to run. Employee turn-over, work attendance and petty theft make these businesses a management headache. I have coached many business owners who were far from happy with their franchise businesses.

In fact, I don't even consider owning a franchise to be business ownership. I consider it as buying yourself a job. Everything you do will be according to the Franchise HQ and policy manual. That sounds pretty much like keeping your boss – only going in debt to keep the boss and in the process, making the boss very rich while you work very hard.

Using your retirement money or your equity to start a business is really a bad idea – at least 90% of the time. The best option, is a low investment start-up and then reinvest the business earnings back into the business to grow it. Paring down your living expenses so you can live on pensions during start-up is the best option for anyone who is a pensioner.

If the business requires a large amount of start-up capital, be careful. What are you investing in? Is it something that can be liquidated—such as equipment or is it operating costs? If the business isn't worthy of bank money—without signing personal guarantees—or it isn't worthy of your money.

Yes, I know banks rarely lend money to a new business without a personal guarantee. That is because they know the risks. If the bank won't risk it—should you?

After all, who has the most leverage, you or the bank? It is far better to find a business opportunity that requires a minimal investment. Incorporate the business. This protects your personal finances should the business fail. The incorporation becomes a separate entity (almost like creating another person) and the business carries its own liabilities without it transferring to the individual.

Banks almost always, even if you incorporate, make you sign a personal guarantee in order to borrow money and sometimes even to operate as a Visa or MasterCard merchant. Some major suppliers may require personal guarantees before granting credit for large amounts of inventory.

Watch the fine print. If you sign a personal guarantee, you become responsible for the liability—you have in effect undone the effectiveness of your incorporation process. Once you sign a personal guarantee, the only value your incorporation may provide is from other liabilities and/or lawsuits where you have not signed a personal guarantee.

How seriously does this need to be considered? I once worked as a Career Transition Coach in government-funded Job Clubs for unemployed mature workers and unemployed professionals. I coached many people who had it made and lost it all. Business mistakes topped the list; second was bad stock market investments and lastly was unexpected medical expenses from traveling without proper medical insurance.

A couple of the medical insurance fiascos came from people who failed to follow the reporting protocol in their policy and had their claims rejected. Another was because the insurance company verified preexisting health conditions that made the insurance invalid. Insurance can also be void if you take what the insurance company deems as *inappropriate risk*—listed in the fine print.

Even if you do not invest personal funds into the business, the need to live off your nest-egg while launching the business may be riskier than working at a paying job with a lower salary. Maybe there is a better business opportunity that doesn't require the same risk.

Watching Dragon's Den or Shark Tank is a good way to get an understanding of how investors assess an investment. Often they invest in the individual. Beyond that they are looking at income potential and they do not get caught up in the emotional pull of the business concept.

Having a business idea that is a good idea—but not a money maker is an easy trap to get caught up in. Sometimes entrepreneurs love their idea and continue to invest time and money into it, even though it is not viable.

Viability has to top the list. If the business concept or product is not viable, no amount of hard work will make it a winner. You can throw good money, at a bad investment forever, without being able to convert it into something viable.

Once you crack the piggy bank, the savings are as good as gone. It is like having a fifty-dollar bill in your wallet or having ten fives. Most people will keep that fifty-dollar bill and know exactly how much is in their wallet.

If they have ten fives, they are more likely to purchase a coffee or trivial items frittering away the fives. Most people who have ten fives could not say with certainty whether they have $40, $45 or $50. Some may even think because the ten fives are bulkier that they have even more than $50.

Living the Entrepreneurial Dream

Successful entrepreneurs don't take blind risks—they take calculated risks. The biggest risk of all is if you are already in a dicey situation as far as retirement capital is concerned and you risk it assuming *nothing ventured, nothing gained.* Know what your contingency plan is. Considering your number of productive years left, do you feel absolutely confident that you will recoup your losses—should the business go south?

Enter any business or self-employment opportunity with a strong dose of realism. Work with a coach. Explore the overall impact on your lifestyle and finances. Develop a plan and stick to it. Projected income statements can sink you. They are often overly optimistic. Be sure your calculations are based on something more than perceived market share. Your market share may be zero, if you do not have a concrete plan as to how you will capture a share of the market.

Planning for Entrepreneurship

Take the appropriate steps to prepare your financial plan if you are going into an entrepreneurial venture. Here are some tips and questions worth asking:

- Figure out the opportunity cost – what will you be sacrificing in each area of your life?
- Cost of replacement of benefits if you are leaving your corporate job and how you can cover these costs.
- Do you really have a big enough financial cushion to make this move?
- What are your choices in mitigating your risks and is it a good business decision?

Do a break-even analysis and projected income statements and then look at your worst case scenario. Most people in start-up stage are overly optimistic. Present your calculations to a neutral third party, such as an accountant or a business coach. Ask them if your case is strong enough that they would invest in it if they were looking for a wise investment. If they wouldn't invest in it, it is likely you shouldn't either.

Can you survive three years, if it takes that long to break even and does it still make sense? If you don't think it will take three years, what are you basing your forecasts on? Do you have existing contracts in your pocket?

What is your contingency plan? Are you motivated by desperation and will your motivation hinder or fuel your success? Panicky people have difficulty maintaining their focus during difficult start-ups.

Can you manage without using RSP's (Canada) or 401K's (US) for financing your business start-up? These funds are dedicated to financing your living expenses, not your business expenses.

Calculate the growth rate of the money if it is invested even at a conservative interest rate and allowed to grow. If siphoning money out of your financial portfolio is going to add to your financial risk in retirement, it may not be the right move. Compounding interest can be more beneficial than self-employed income. $50,000 compounded for 30 years at an average of 8% interest accumulates a balance of $500,000.

Do not use home equity as a source of financing a business start-up or for that matter, anything. Debt free living is the goal in retirement and anything that increases your indebtedness is usually a bad idea.

Mortgage rates have been very low in recent years and countless people have mortgages they could not maintain if the interest inches up even a few percentage points. If you recall the 1980's, you know that interest rates climbed to over 21% on mortgages. It can happen again. Anyone who doesn't think so has their head in the sand. Interest on debt is always higher than interest on savings. You cannot pay debt with your savings interest.

Planning your Launch

Start your plan and save the money in a separate account, until you are in a position where you are able to launch the business and know you will have enough money to live at least one to three years during the start-up phase. Saving money encourages you to look at frugality. You will need to be frugal during business start-up and you are better off to prove you can live frugally in advance of your start-up.

Moderate frugality can be beneficial to all retirees. Learning to cut unnecessary spending can make the difference between living in a state of extreme financial stress and living comfortably. You may protest and say *living frugally isn't living!* However, here is my challenge back to you: *is living with financial stress, living?*

The difference in people who are in good shape financially at retirement is often frugality. If we are brutally honest, we know that there is no direct correlation between income and financial net worth. There are tons of people who have earned over 6 figures most of the last ten years leading up to retirement and who end up with nothing; and there are tons of people who have earned very low incomes by comparison (maybe 1/3 of that income) and they have tidy nest eggs.

The Credit Card Trap

If you have credit cards, you must be creditworthy and capable of paying them—right? Credit card companies rely on your inability to pay the balance down to zero at the end of every month. That is the most costly financial error you can make. Never use a credit card to start a business. We already discussed how impossible it is to pay off credit card debt if you borrow more than you can pay off when you receive your statement.

If you max a credit card out and have difficulty paying it, the interest you will spend will far exceed anything you can generate from even the most successful investment. Even worse, if you are putting something that depreciates, or is expendable on a credit card, the item is gone before the debt is paid.

Putting a sofa for your office, on a department store credit card and pay off the minimum monthly balance, you will end up paying more than the price of a car for your sofa and it can take up to 30 years! I don't know of a sofa that lasts 30 years! Buying your groceries or paying your business operating costs by incurring debt is a surefire way to fail. It is fine to use credit cards for business transactions—but they need to be paid off regularly.

According to the Financial Consumer Agency of Canada, there were 68.6 million credit cards circulating in Canada, or about 2.9 for every adult. Once you start using one credit card to make payments on another, or juggling your utility bills to keep your utilities from being cut off, you have reached the point of no return. Getting financial counseling is far over do.

I am not an investment advisor and cannot give you advice about how to invest your money. There are non-profit debt counseling services that consolidate your debts. Even then, you need to make careful decisions. Refinancing and consolidating your debt may only delay the inevitable if your spending exceeds your income.

Out of Necessity

Many people over 55 start businesses out of necessity. While it may appear that there are lots of jobs, age discrimination certainly exists in many areas and industries. If you are in a position where the only way to stop your unemployment is to employ yourself, do it with prudence. Keep your risks low and be sure you have some income stream quickly from the business start-up. Do your research and unless you have strong previous business ownership experience, seek the help of a business coach.

While coaching may seem like an added expense, it is a question of how quickly you need to become successful. Think of a tennis player. A friend of mine was a tennis coach for more than ten years. He says the choice of whether to hire a coach is clear. "It all depends on how long you have to learn to play the game and how good you want to become."

I don't believe anyone goes into business intending to squeak by, and time is money; Anyone who is considering business start-up will hire a business coach for the same reason a tennis player hires a tennis coach—to become better, sooner. If you are entering your business thinking that as long as you can squeak by, it is good enough, don't start!

Necessity is the Mother of Inspiration

While I have thus far painted a negative picture of entrepreneurship, I believe it is rewarding and viable – when a good plan is in place. The media bombard us with negative stories, and inspirational stories are not shared nearly enough. What do you do when the house of cards falls and you find your life in a crisis? How do you even dare to think about retirement?

Your vulnerability has been experienced and the uncertainty of how the future will look is palpable. People who hit retirement without any vision of what they are going to do with their time and energy beyond retirement can experience this kind of disorientation. But the feeling of disorientation can become overwhelming when accident or sudden debilitating injury undermines the way you planned to live your retirement.

This is what happened to Jan. She and her husband had married 13 years ago - a second marriage for both of them. They had a wonderful retirement plan, but something beyond their control derailed it. Jan had spent much of her career as an Elementary School Principal and as she neared retirement, she was the Director of Professional Development for the county government and school system near her home.

She long recognized the challenge for educators, teachers and principals. “Retiring from a job in the education system is like leaving a monastery. In the school system, everything is so dictated. There is the recess bell, the bell between classes, the exam timetable, the curriculum and school holidays. Your life is completely structured and very few choices are made by you as an individual. It is like leaving the litany of a church and finding out now you have to make all the decisions yourself with no one to guide you.”

Bob, her husband, had been a Career Naval Officer for 20 years. Jan and Bob intended to spend their early retirement years teaching at the local university. That was until ten days prior to retirement. A severe rear-end car accident altered their plan. As with most rear-end collisions, it takes time before the severity of the soft tissue damage manifests its effects. It can take a very long time before the final outcome becomes obvious.

For Jan, severe soft tissue damage from the whiplash and the injuries sustained from the restraint of the seatbelt left her emotionally disoriented. It was suddenly obvious that life as she had known it had ended. Her retirement plans seemed unachievable, and it turned into a difficult time.

"All the things you take for granted in life are suddenly gone. Then you have aging parents to deal with at the same time and it creates a domino effect as you struggle to make sense of the situation—everything seems to tumble down," says Jan. She struggled to make sense of what life in retirement would now look like.

"My business venture began serendipitously as I sought to find a way to keep my mind active and keep from feeling too sorry for myself. Even before retirement, I thrived on anything creative. I felt in some ways that the creative side of me was subverted during my career. As I thought I would put more energy into my painting, I wanted photos to paint. So I started taking photos as I was out walking. I soon learned that when I was doing something creative, I was more able to cope with what I was going through and it was easier to forget my pain."

"I realized it was time to let the Creative Genie out of the box. I started going through photos I already had on my computer and loved playing around with the photos of nature and soon felt like I was taking back control of my life."

Jan says she is not a salesperson and never wants to become one. It wasn't too long until Bob, recognizing the therapeutic benefits Jan derived from working with the photos, asked to be signed up as the "CFO of an organization of two," Jan says. "He was an amateur artist himself. We are self-taught and still learning. Each time you take a photo, even from the same spot, the lighting changes, the seasons and weather change and it is a new opportunity to use all those elements to your advantage for the new photo."

Jan attributes much of her healing to the beauty of nature. "Something just happens to you when you are standing at the top of a mountain on a beautiful calm windless day. You can't help breathing differently. All the anxiety stops and you see the world and everything differently from that vantage point. It is a kind of meditation if you will."

Their business was born.

They specialize in creating boutique quality note cards, greeting cards, postcards, prints, DVDs, calendars, screen savers and montage posters featuring their unique photography. Jan and Bob spend their days taking photos of the hazy greens of summer, the russets and golds of autumn, the grays, whites and blues of winter, and the fragile greens and pinks of Virginia's springs.

Their business evolves through word of mouth and they don't have any aspirations of growing it beyond what it is. Sometimes things come their way that takes their enjoyment and fulfillment to another level. After working at their little business together and enjoying it immensely, Bob had his own brush with serious health issues. He underwent a triple bypass surgery. It was a very stressful time.

Two months after he returned home from his surgery, they received a phone call from the medical centre where Bob had his surgery. The caller told them that he had seen their work and had been doing a lot of reading about healing environments and had invited Jan and Bob to provide all the artwork for a new Cardiac Transition Unit.

At the time, the centre did not understand that Bob had just undergone his own bypass surgery at the facility. Jan and Bob sorted through their photos and presented a selection for the medical centre to review. The staff and administrators chose 30 photos. The photos were then enlarged to poster size and framed.

The beautiful scenery photos taken by Jan and Bob offer an environment that "causes the viewer to connect with peace and take a deep breath. Even if we had no other business success, this one opportunity to impact people who are facing the same anxieties as we faced not too many months ago ourselves, makes it all worth it. It is so good to think our photos will give people an opportunity to take a more serene view and a deep breath when they need it most."

From simple beginnings and an ability to connect with Jan's creative side, this business venture gives this couple fulfillment and joy.

It didn't come from an easy beginning. Jan said, "You have heard it said when life hands you lemons make lemonade, but when the domino effect has destroyed your plans, it is even hard to know how to do that." The power of this story is that what starts as a small step in a recovery process can lead to something meaningful. No matter where you are today—there is the possibility—allowing the creativity within you to shine through can open new doors. The power of *possibility thinking* changes lives, society and our world. However, possibility thinking must be combined with positive doing.

The life you create for yourself is yours to enjoy as you celebrate your strengths and seize your opportunities. Life is an ongoing process of character development—you are the hero of your life.

CHAPTER 14

IGNITING THE POWER OF INTENT:

AN EXERCISE IN LIVING WELL

Living well is the best revenge.

George Herbert (1593 – 1633)

It is easy to underestimate the power of longevity and future opportunities. It is equally easy to fail to credit ourselves for days lived well. We can become oblivious to the passing of our days without investing in living them well. Time is in many ways an abstract commodity. It is, as we know, the easiest thing to waste and it is impossible to redeem once we have wasted it.

If we could depict the days of our lives in a more tangible visual way, perhaps we would connect, more fully, with how we are living our lives. With this in mind, I have created a visual concept and a ritual that can keep you aware of how you are living on a daily basis. By renewing your commitment to live life well, each and every day, and by acknowledging days lived well, you can create a powerful habit that will enable you to take your life to unprecedented levels of achievement, joy and meaning.

This concept has an artistic twist that is within the reach of even those who see themselves as not creatively inclined and can be as spectacular as you want to make it. The objective is to build a *Life Clock***.**

The Life Clock will provide a visual impact helping you to relate with how BIG life is. The Life Clock will portray your future and help you assess how you live on a day-to-day basis. The process will encourage you to live each day to its fullest—making for many good days. Quantifying the number of good days you have will help reinforce the mentality that *life is good.*

Too many people over 50 are trapped between a sense of urgency – life is running out and a state of paralysis – "I'll get around to it next month, I am too busy right now." Often days fill without much to show for our time.

Time is our greatest opportunity factor. Even three years is 1,095 days – that is a lot of time. Thirty years is 10,950 days.

Change your Life in 100 Days

A new perspective of time was granted to me a few years back. My 21 year old daughter took a trip around the world. Had she only traveled around the world, she would have logged 24,900 miles. However, she crisscrossed China, Mongolia and many other countries, taking her many more miles. One hundred days later, to the day, she returned having seen most of Asia, Europe, and Scandinavia.

During those 100 days, her grandmother lost 36 pounds. Some personal goals I had set were left incomplete – others were completed. I spent most of my time writing a book. As I reflected on those 100 days, I was satisfied with how I had spent them.

At 21 my daughter had completed a four year degree, travelled around the world, and returned to do graduate studies. She achieved it all on scholarships and her own efforts to save money from co-op work assignments. What leaves the biggest impression for me, is that my daughter wrote this goal in a journal when she was only 12 years old. Right down to seeing the Panda breeding center in China—she carried through.

Her grandmother lost the weight – because of a decision that she needed to address her health challenges. For me, writing was a decision to embark on a massive personal growth process for myself – and to make a difference in the lives of others – my core source of life meaning.

All of this is a snippet of time – 100 days. Where will you be in your next 100 days? If that is what is possible in 100 days what is possible in 10,950 or 14,600 days?

The BIG Picture

We are going to do a little exercise. How many years do you potentially have left? Figure out how many days you have to live based on life expectancy plus 10 or 15 years – or be bold and choose age 105. Now multiply that by 365. That is how many days you could have left.

I suggest choosing an age significantly older than today's life expectancy, as life expectancy rates increase every ten years, due to medical breakthroughs and preventative health education.

It is highly likely that within the next 20 to 30 years life expectancy could increase by ten or fifteen years. Furthermore, it isn't my objective to make you feel at any point, that you are running out of time – creating a greater sense of urgency.

As a coach, I have discovered that many people are living their lives believing they will die younger than the life expectancy figures indicate – or they accept life expectancy as a finite END. What most people forget is that life expectancy is an average.

For everyone that predeceases the life expectancy age, another person will out-live the life expectancy age. Your life expectancy actually rises as you outlive others, as you become one of the people who help counterbalance the early deaths that drag averages down. According to Statistics Canada if you live to 80, your life expectancy raises to 2.17 years beyond the *life expectancy at birth figures* we most often use when talking about life expectancy.

While inevitably, we become more aware of our mortality as we age, a fatalistic mentality has to become, at least to some extent, a self-fulfilling prophecy. In life, we already know we never achieve more than what we believe to be possible—therefore, aim high.

Creating the Life Clock

The Life Clock consists of clear glass vases and small gems. The size of the gem you choose will determine the size of your Life Clock. Your living space and budget can take this all the way from small, inexpensive beads to fresh water pearls or polished pebbles. Other options are pennies, pea-gravel, marbles, or floral vase gems (flat marbles). It could be a focal point of a room—or a smaller, simple display. Choose a different color gem for each ten years. You can be as creative as you want. My suggestion is, this is symbolic of your life—so go BIG and make it BEAUTIFUL.

Each gem is symbolic of a day. You will be starting with all the gems in the *Future Days* vase. You will need two empty vases, to transfer the gems into as you live your days. One of the empty vases, the larger one, will be *Days Well Lived;* the smaller empty vase will be *Lost Days* – days that fall short of your expectations for a meaningful *Inspirement.*

The Lost Days are days you would rather forget—days where the problems, challenges and disappointments outweighed the redeeming qualities of the time spent. Lost Days to be relegated to small places in our memory—as dwelling on what didn't go well is counterproductive to wellbeing. The aim is to keep the Lost Days vase from filling. As life passes, your Days Well Lived vase will fill-up and leave the Future Days vase emptying.

As you retire each night, move one gem into either the Days Well Lived vase, or the Lost Days vase. You can even use your Life Clock for measuring the progress of a personal project – such as *days I succeeded in maintaining my exercise regime*. The motivation is always to keep from adding to the Lost Days vase.

Setting up the Life Clock

Step 1. Figure out what you need. Purchase or find enough items to tally the number of days left. Thirty years will require 10,950 gems. Forty years will require 14,600 gems.

Depending on the size of the gems, a very large vase for your display, as you need enough vases to hold all the gems, plus two empty vases—which can be smaller.

Dollar store spaghetti storage jars work if you use 1/8 inch beads and are affordable. Dollar stores may be a good source for your gems or other suitable items. The next best place to shop would be a craft store.

<u>*Step 2:*</u> As we are not fixated on accuracy, it isn't necessary to count every gem. Figure out approximately how many fit in a cup and then do the math to figure out the volume of gems needed to

depict your Future Years and how many vases you will need.

To do my initial calculation, I counted the number of uncooked white beans that fit in a small scoop and figured that about one cup is the equivalent of four years. Therefore, using small items, such as beads or fresh water pearls (if you want to splurge) would require 10 cups of beads.

Unless you intend this to be a sizeable display, using something small like fresh water pearls or beads is the best choice. Based on fresh water pearls (about the same size as the white beans) it would take about three large vases (3–4 inches in diameter and 12 -15 inches tall). Varying the size of the vases will make the display more artistic and visually appealing. Colored glass floral vase gems could create a spectacular display although this would require very large decorator vases.

My Future Days vase is approximately 10 inches in diameter and 30 inches tall. It is stunning. I used two large spaghetti jars (4" x 24" and 4" x 18") for my Days Well Lived and my Lost Days vases. I used 90% small blue flat marbles–sometimes called floral gems (3/8" size) and 10% regular floral gems

(1/2”). I chose bluc tones, clear, and a few light violet. Pouring them in by color in layers added to the beauty of it. I use the larger floral gems for spectacular days–such as book launches, family events such as graduations or weddings, and smaller gems for day-to-day days that went well. I will use the violet gems for ‘my darker’ days—Lost Days.

My Days Lived Well vase is a 12” x 3” spaghetti storage jar, and it holds about 5 years of gems. I may need to add another vase as time passes, until my smallest Future Days vase empties and becomes a place to store my Days Well Lived.

My Lost Days vase is a 6” x 3” a shorter version, of the spaghetti jar. I anticipate it will take more than 10 years or to fill it. My Life Clock sits on my fireplace mantel and is a spectacular sight. Where you choose to display your Life Clock depends on whether young children visit your home. The gems could present a choking hazard.

Step 3: Set up the display in a prominent place: on your dresser; the living room; the fireplace mantel or on a hall table. Mentally or otherwise label the vases. Place a label on the back of the Future Days vase showing the date the clock started and with a promise to yourself, or what you intend to do with your life – and sign it. It is very important that the vases are easily identified otherwise as the volume of the vases begins equalizing it would be easy to become confused.

Step 4: Each time you place a gem in the Days Well Lived vase, pause a moment and reflect on all the things that made it a great day. Do not aim for perfection. Any day can count as well lived, as long as it fits your expectations for a meaningful *Inspirement.* Promise yourself to live tomorrow to the fullest. If you have a day when everything seemed to go wrong, and need to place a gem in the Lost Days vase, reflect on how you can ensure that tomorrow will be a better day. This exercise will mentally reinforce *positive thinking* and *positive doing*. Complacency cannot set in if you ignite the power of intention every day. Keep the fire stoked and burning. Living life to the fullest can become a habit.

If you are going away for a holiday, take pill bottles filled with uncooked white beans and two empty pill bottles labeled to identify the Days Well Lived and Lost Days. Continue to keep track and then adjust your Life Clock on your arrival back home.

Step 5: On the monthly anniversary of the day you started this Life Clock, reflect on the number of positive days you have spent, since starting. Reflect on the Future Days vase and resolve to make them worthwhile. If you feel the number of Lost Days are stacking up too quickly, it's time to work with a coach for a while to get you back on the path to creating the *Inspirement* you desire.

I find my guests and family can't resist my Life Clock and frequently will go to my Life Clock and play with the gems. At first, I was quite possessive of my Life Clock and felt like it needed a 'do not disturb' sign on it. However, I quickly realized—these are people who want to be part of my future. They are people who will share those future days with me.

Inevitably, if you do this exercise for a minimum of three months, the habit will be as ingrained as brushing your teeth and the results can be phenomenal. Each day you are committing to living life to the fullest. Isn't that what we really want? Can you imagine the possibilities?

CHAPTER 15

CONCLUSION:

IT'S NOT OVER YET

I look to the future because that's where I'm going to spend the rest of my life.

George Burns (1896 - 1996)

Adopt the belief that the best is yet to come! Why settle for less? It is far from over; we are middle-aged. Half of our life is ahead of us. We have wisdom and experience that will enable us to accomplish things we could not accomplish earlier in life. Living the life you want instead of settling for what you think you *have to do* is the ticket to retiring with panache.

If you observe the life stories of many people who have made major contributions to their profession or to society in general, it is often apparent the last 10 to 20 years of their life is where they made the biggest discoveries, contributions or accomplishments.

What have you accomplished in the past twenty years? What would you like to accomplish in the next twenty? Where we are today is vastly different than we imagined when we left high school. The next thirty or forty years of our lives is an open door – leading to many choices.

The future is ours to enjoy. The option of embracing opportunities and experiences are only limited by our ability to conceive the ideas and to bring them into being. As we plan for our future, our plan needs to be a living document –evolving as new goals are achieved and as new opportunities present themselves.

We are retiring in a unique time in history. The world is smaller than ever, through convenient travel, global economies and technology possibilities we couldn't even conceive as recently as twenty years ago.

Think back to the hippie era. Our ability to imagine the changes that have come about was at best limited. Even as we embark on our journey forward—it requires the cumulative sum of all our imaginations to envision the world of 2050. Our tendency is to imagine something not that much different from today. The reality is the society and world of 2050, will be created by the steady evolution created by people who are not willing to settle for mediocrity or complacency.

It isn't over yet!

It has just begun!

References:

Statistics Canada (1996),

Family Caregivers Association

Families Caring for an Aging America. Authors: Committee on Family Caregiving for Older Adults; Board on Health Care Services; Health and Medicine Division; National Academies of Sciences, Engineering, and Medicine.

The Partnership to Fight Chronic Disease: www.fightchronicdisease.org/sites/default/files/docs/Almanac_Final

Recognizing and Treating Depression: A Guide for the Elderly and Their Caregivers By Richard Boyle

The Journal of the American Medical Association, December 15, 1999, Vol. 282, No. 23,

American Psychological Association: The High Cost of Caregiving :

Long-term Care Financing:
Growing Demand and Cost of Services Are Straining Federal and State Budgets
Gao-05-564t: Published: Apr 27, 2005.

Volunteering is Associated with Delayed Mortality in Older People: Analysis of the Longitudinal Study of Aging

Alex H. S. Harris, Carl E. Thoresen First Published December 1, 2005 Research Article Find in PubMed https://doi.org/10.1177/1359105305057310

Dr. Tsai and colleagues in the British Journal of Medicine

Manufactured by Amazon.ca
Bolton, ON